OCTOBER '43

Aage Bertelsen

TRANSLATED BY MILLY LINDHOLM
AND WILLY AGTBY WITH A FOREWORD
BY *Sholem Asch*

G. P. PUTNAM'S SONS New York

Foreword

BY SHOLEM ASCH
(Translated by Maurice Samuel)

Let me state at the outset that this book deals with one of the unhappiest chapters in the modern history of mankind; nevertheless it is not a sad book but a joyous one, a book not of human degradation but of human exaltation. For it is a book not of hatred but of the noblest form of love which man is capable of demonstrating. I would call it the Book of the Great Psalm of Praise, an ode to the human species. Between these two covers are lodged the hopes and the comfort which sustain you and me, and sustain all mankind.

You and I need the word of comfort, of hope and of faith in man. Over our heads hangs a sword of terror —terror of our brother-man. Who is he, this brother-man? And what is he? Is that which has happened in our day, and before our eyes, this self-stripping on the part of man, this self-denuding of human attributes, this relapse into animalism—is it an exceptional incident, a tragic episode in the development of human history? Or is it the assertion of a fundamental characteristic, a return to that inveterate bestiality which we had falsely persuaded ourselves had been eradicated by the processes of culture and civilization? One is compelled to think of an unsuccessful experiment in cross-breeding, in which the new type, apparently well established, relapses into the undesirable original: in this instance man, after millennia of Judaeo-Greek-Christian "cross-breeding," collapsed to the original primitive beast. Who could tell whether that which had happened in our generation might not recur in the next or the next but one? And should this indeed be the case, of what avail and to what purpose is all our agony and our striving? We are enclosed in the iron ring of a destiny which cannot be broken.

Bitter and heavy as was the physical catastrophe which came on the Jewish people and on all the other victims of the Nazi assassins, equally bitter and heavy (and perhaps more so) was the moral catastrophe which overtook the German people. And not the German people alone. Let us be honest with ourselves: all mankind has been involved in this chain of sin. It has happened in our day, and it is in our times that we must look for the causes which made possible the calamity we have witnessed.

Our generation, the generation placed between the

two wars, carries its burden of guilt: the generation which looked on at the suppression of the human personality and the desecration of its sanctities, first by the creators of communism as a means to a materialist end, then by the creators of Nazism, as a means to an exploitative overlordship; the generation of a material and moral inflation which cast aside all the ancient truths and became indifferent to the ghastly spectacle of the moral nakedness of man.

All things have their causes, and a generation which produced these incidents and circumstances carries the responsibility for them, just as the individual is responsible for his actions. The crushing burden of the times lies upon all of us, on the smitten as well as the smiters, and even more on the "neutrals," the spectators and bystanders: all of us may utter the cry of the psalmist: "Out of the depths I cry unto Thee, O God. Bring us back our hope and our faith in ourselves."

It is therefore of the highest importance not only to record and recount, both for ourselves and for the future, the evidences of human degradation, but side by side with them to set forth the evidences of human exaltation and of nobility. Let the epic of heroic deeds of love, as opposed to those of hatred, of rescue as opposed to destruction, bear equal witness to the unborn generations.

This book is not the work of a single person. It was written by an entire people, from its highest citizen, old and noble King Christian X, who took from his head the glorious crown of Denmark and set it upon the bloodstained head of the Jewish victim when he elected to wear the sign of death, the Jewish Shield of David, on his breast, to the humblest fisherman who risked his life in his little boat helping to save thousands of Jews from the murderous Nazis. It is written not in words but in deeds, performed under supreme peril to life and limb.

Hitler destroyed six million Jews; it is not inaccurate to say that he destroyed the whole of European Jewry. Only a tiny fragment survived. Some, through miraculous escapes, emerged from the concentration camps to which they had been consigned with the gas chambers as their ultimate destination. Others found a hiding place in the underground, in churches and among village peasants; some in the homes of city dwellers. Of all these it may be said that they owed their lives to Christians.

Let it be granted that various motives were at play. It may be recorded that many took payment from those they rescued, or rather exacted the last possible reward from the wretched victims. But if all these are added up, they still constitute a small minority compared with those who were actuated by purely humanitarian and religious motives. Never, as long as human records endure, will the world forget the Catholic priests and nuns who put their lives in jeopardy—and in many instances made the supreme sacrifice—to rescue Jewish children from death. In this heroic enterprise we shall find almost every European people among which there was a Jewish community. Even in Germany, heart and fount of the Nazi abomination, there were, according to Martin Buber and others, magnificent instances of this kind. The heroes were drawn from every stratum; the larger part, however—and this is particularly true of France—belonged to the village populations.

But no country has achieved in this respect the glorious distinction of little Denmark. It is accurate to say that in proportion to the number of the Jews in its midst Denmark stands out among the countries of Europe, first without a second; for the rescue comprised almost the entire Jewish population. The "Jewish Dunkirk" carried out by Denmark would have been impossible if it had not enlisted the passionate cooperation of every level of the population, and if it had not been animated by the spirit so clearly expressed by one of the heroes of the story, who, asked by the author of this book to cooperate with him, answered: "That's O.K. . . . I don't know much about Jews, but this is bloody well against my religion and my morals—hunting people as if they were rats."

It is obvious that Denmark could never have carried out this gigantic rescue operation without the help of Sweden, which opened its frontiers to the Jewish refugees. On the flood of sin, hatred and blood which Hitler let loose upon the world there swam a small ark which preserved intact the common heritage of a

Judaeo-Christian outlook, that outlook which is founded on the double principle of love of God and love of one's fellow man. The demonism of Hitler had sought to overturn the ark and to overwhelm it in the floods of hate. It was saved by the heroism of a handful of saints. Let us now release from the ark the goodness which was preserved from destruction, let us spread it about the earth. This, indeed, is the purpose of Aage Bertelsen's book, which seeks to breathe into man a new faith in himself and new hope for the future.

For this book must not be regarded simply as a document for the historians of coming generations. It is an all-human book of the highest value, a record of the behavior of man in the hour of supreme trial, and under the shadow of death. It differs from the great majority of books on the great catastrophe in one important respect: the latter were written for the most part by men who walked in the valley of the shadow of death, not of their own free will. Their records are touched with the personal anguish of the search for rescue; they bring with them the breath of the gas chambers.

This however is the record of one who, though he risked death a hundred times, and knew danger as an intimate, was himself not among the condemned. It was by choice, not by compulsion, that he found himself under the ban, and because his action was dictated by calm determination, he was able to observe with a sober eye the behavior of those who were under sentence of death. But this sobriety of observation must not be confused with indifference. There is a continuous overtone of sympathy and understanding for the sufferers; more than that, there is a passion of apologetics, streaming from the purest sources of human love. His observations are of the deepest value for students of psychology. Such, for instance, is his description of the manner in which the persecuted cling in the hour of deadly need to the minutest details of their religious ritual, and increase the danger of their situation a hundredfold in order to carry out their ceremonial. Let no one call this a senseless fetishism; it is an expression of the ineradicable belief in God, overriding the last agonies of fear; it is a refusal to cut one's self off from the ultimate hope of man.

The book unfolds a gallery of unforgettable characters and personalities, both among the persecuted Jews and among the great-hearted Christians who come to their rescue; and it is written with a penetration which rises to artistic heights. In the midst of the tragedy and despair there breathes a light humor which refreshes the spirit, and makes us forget the horror of the situation. The scenes in which the author, who is risking his life to rescue the victims of Nazism, is transformed by those victims into a *Shabbos-Goy*, are extraordinarily authentic for my people.

I offer you my thanks, Aage Bertelsen, for having

collected these episodes as one would collect pearls for a necklace. You have produced an ornament to humanity. Hitler had set himself as an ideal the total sundering of Christian from Jew. Books like yours defeat his purpose, unite and bind up, bring together and create a whole between faith and faith, between one people and another.

Like an old Jewish peddler our father Abraham bargained and haggled with God over the fate of Sodom and Gomorrah: *"Perhaps there will be found five just men in the city . . ."* So we too must bargain and haggle in our own day, but with ourselves, in order to sustain our faith in mankind. This is what Aage Bertelsen's book helps us to do.

Contents

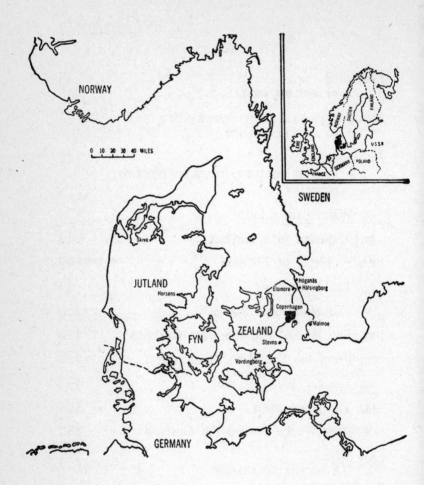

NORWAY

0 10 20 30 40 MILES

SWEDEN

Skive

JUTLAND

Horsens

Høganäs

Elsinore Halsingborg

Copenhagen

ZEALAND

Malmoe

FYN

Stevns

Vordingborg

GERMANY

Introduction to the American Edition

BY AAGE BERTELSEN

THIS is a book about things that happened in a small country during World War II. To some extent it may be considered unimportant in today's world. What we experienced during those years soon lost interest after the literary overproduction of the first postwar years, and it is only natural that, in the age of the Cold War, we should prefer to forget what happened during those years of horror.

However, some readers have thought that all the same my little book might prove of interest even outside Denmark, not only because it deals with a problem which seems to be of eternal and dreadful actuality—the persecution of our Jewish fellow men—but mostly because of the special conditions tied up with the pogroms in my native country. For although through two thousand years of the history of mankind such oppression has resulted in a sea of blood and tears, the story of Hitler's persecution of the Jews in Denmark is well qualified to strike a softer note in our minds despite the traditional features of horror and terror. Everybody knows that during their rule in Germany and the other countries occupied by Hitler, the Nazis sent five million Jews to the gas-chambers. But this book is the story of how a small nation, terrorized by the Germans, nevertheless rallied against the man hunters and sent our six to seven thousand Jews, including both citizens and others who had sought refuge within our frontiers, to safety and freedom in our Swedish brother-country.

How was this possible? It should be mentioned first of all that to a great extent it is due to the favorable position of our country, encircled by the sea as it is. The Sound, which separates Denmark from Sweden, is a comparatively narrow channel, though deep and with strong and capricious currents that make it dangerous to navigate with boats and small vessels on a dark autumn night. In one place the distance between the two shores is not more than three miles. Add to this that the coastline of Zealand is rather long and difficult to control effectively. So there is hardly any doubt that in Denmark we had a better chance to help the persecuted Jews than had their friends in other countries, provided that the means necessary for such sudden and comprehensive transport of refugees could be obtained.

When Sweden, one of the few countries in Europe to stay neutral and unoccupied, opened her arms to the refugees with a matter-of-course hospitality, it was equally natural to most Danes that we should help the Jews to the utmost of our ability. The will to do so was strong, though at that time we felt that our abilities and the chances of success were few and far between. The coast was guarded as closely as possible by the German police, and all private boats and ships had long ago been removed from Danish shores by order, for the purpose of preventing illegal crossings to Sweden. No real preparations could be made for mass escapes, among other things because the persecution started almost completely without warning and with no preliminary measures against the Jews, such as served as warnings in other countries of what was going to take place. It is true that since August 29, 1943, when the Germans deposed the King and dismissed the lawful government and parliament, there had been rumors that a persecution of the Jews was to be expected. But so far all reports and conjectures of that kind had proved unfounded, so when in the days before the first of October the Jews were informed of what to expect in the near future there were several who could not, or would not, believe that this time it was true. Consequently, these were caught by the Gestapo.

All the work in connection with the escape of the Jews had to be improvised under very difficult and dangerous circumstances, and it would hardly have proved possible to carry it through had not the active helpers of the Jews been helped by the majority of the Danish people, directly or indirectly. A certain knowledge of the Danes and their country, and of its modern history, will consequently be necessary to form a background for the understanding of what took place in October, 1943.

Denmark is a small country, one of the smallest in Europe, with about four million inhabitants. With nearly 500 islands, of which Zealand with the capital city of Copenhagen is the largest, Denmark is completely encircled by the sea. Her coast is about 5,500 miles long, and to the north and the east she faces Norway and Sweden. In the west we have the "Mainland" of Jutland, contiguous with Germany but with a coastline along the North Sea facing Great Britain and beyond that faraway U.S.A.

The nature of the country has formed the mind and temperament of the people. The sea gives us a mild insular climate and the outlines of the country-side in the islands and eastern Jutland are undulating and friendly, an idyll of woods and lakes, with rounded hills and a bounteous soil. However, there are also the considerable heights and the wide expanses of Central and Western Jutland and the stern magnitude of the North Sea to be reckoned with.

As a whole the Danish people live under good conditions, thanks to our well-cultivated soil, a highly developed agriculture, a shipping and commercial trade relatively among the biggest in the world, and industries which, despite lack of raw materials, are able to compete with foreign ones because of the high quality of their products. There is no stratification of society of any importance, and the difference between rich and poor is less than in most other countries. During the century in which we have had a free political constitution, a democratic way of thinking has penetrated deeply into the mind of the Danes. "A man is a man even if he is not bigger than a mouse," is the common Danish wording of the declaration on human rights.

That is the reason why there has been no problem of racial antagonism and no strong religious contrasts in Denmark. Before the war the Danish Jews lived just like other Danes, more or less attached to the synagogue in Copenhagen or with no connection with the Jewish religion at all. Most frequently the majority of their fellow citizens took no notice of the differences in appearance or religion. The possibility of special legislation governing the Jews was, and is, completely incompatible with the Danish way of thinking, and in Denmark—unlike the practice in many other places in Europe—there has never been a "ghetto" or special streets reserved for our Jewish countrymen. We have and have had outstanding Jews in our spiritual life, in literature, science, art, public education, and in business. But with a few exceptions in literature they have not made their Jewish, distinctive features felt. For more than a hundred years there has been an increasing tendency toward assimilation in the relation between the Jews and the other Danes, even as Zionism has met with growing approval and sympathy from both quarters. Not until the outbreak of Nazism in Germany can it be said that a real Jewish problem came into existence in Denmark. It should be noted, however, that even then most Danes had only contempt and scorn for anti-Jewish sentiments. The only exception was an insignificant minority, infected by the anti-Semitic madness from the south.

Through the entire history of Denmark our relationship with our neighbors, the great German people, has been decisive for us for good or evil. Our linguistic, literary, and religious development has been under constant influence from other countries, and within these fields Denmark is deeply indebted to the German language and culture. From a political point of view Jutland's geographical connection with Germany has caused conflicts between Danes and Germans in the border area, which have led to bloody wars. In 1864 we lost the southern part of Jutland, Schleswig, after a war which reached its climax in one of the bloodiest battles of modern martial history, that at the Dybboel earthworks. This dismembering of our country was the first result of the political maxim expressed by Bismarck in his famous sentence, "Great policy is not made by decisions of the majority or by speeches, but by blood and iron." This cynical confession that might makes right has ever since been borne out in German political matters, through the wars with Austria in 1866 and with France in 1870 up to the conclusion of World War I in 1918, and it was given its freest scope during the Nazi dictatorship and terror, with the suppression of free and peace-loving peoples in World War II—including the Danish people.

On April 9, 1940, Denmark was occupied by the German *Wehrmacht*. Like a thief in the night, with no warning at all, the German army and navy sneaked across the Danish frontier and coasts. After a short fight in Southern Jutland (North Schleswig), which had been recaptured after World War I, we surrendered to crushingly superior forces. What later happened was not only a political occupation but also a brutal breach of promise, and of cowardice unparalleled. A few months previously Germany herself had forced upon us a "pact of friendship." For a great part of the Danish population this blow came as an earthquake, shaking our very view on life: such things could happen to us, too. The belief in justice, and in the inner strength of humanity and freedom, which to many of us formed an inalienable background for our democratic outlook on life, was shaken to its foundations by this underhand attack on our country. And just as in 1864 it became true

9

that the German rule of violence of our small nation became the first link in a fatal, world-wide chain reaction; within the following weeks Norway, too, submitted to superior Teutonic forces after heroic fighting, and in the following months Holland, Belgium, France.

Denmark submitted herself to the severe regulations of necessity. The Danish King and government were allowed to go on governing subject to German control, and they adjusted their politics in order to alleviate the gravest outrages of this regime of violence, so utterly strange to the nature and the way of thinking of the Danish people, and so completely incompatible with our political traditions.

In the long run this paradoxical relationship proved impossible. The constant conflicts between Germans and Danes led to a situation when, in the end, sabotage against Danish enterprises working for the interests of Germany and the German counter-sabotage developed into a definite warlike rebellion. On August 29, 1943, after an ultimatum to the Danish government headed by Mr. Erik Scavenius —who rejected the ultimatum—the *Wehrmacht* struck. The Danish garrisons in Copenhagen and the provincial towns were imprisoned, or beaten where they fought back, the Royal Navy sank itself or shaped a course for Sweden. The King was caught after an armed attack on his palace, Sorgenfri near Lyngby, the cabinet was dismissed and parliament

10

dissolved. The daily management of the governing of the country was placed in the hands of the leaders of the Danish administration (a so-called management by the heads of the individual departments) on the instigation and with the approval of the King and the government. Dr. Best, Hitler's plenipotentiary, became the highest authority in the country.

But the effects of the action of August 29 fell short of German expectations. Hitler's "model protectorate" was changed to an ever-increasing degree into a country at war, a land of terror, just like Norway, Holland, and other occupied countries, and "this ridiculous, small nation," as Dr. Best called it, developed during the years preceding the Liberation a resistance movement which Field Marshal Montgomery characterized in terms of honor: second to none. The blowing up of Danish factories working for the Germans, sabotage against the railways to impede communications with Germany, and all conceivable kinds of real and symbolic resistance against the German spirit and German methods, were countered with terror, transportation to German concentration camps, torture in the chambers of the Gestapo, and executions of many Danish saboteurs.

The night of the 1st-2nd October was the night set for the German raid on the Danish Jews. It was launched in accordance with orders direct from Hitler, dictated by his rage at the heavily increased resistance in Denmark. As so often in history those in power now resorted to the expedient we know so well: to let the Jewish people become the scapegoat, to make up for their own hatred, their fear, and their disappointments.

Here again the Biblical picture of "the thief in the night" fits in nicely yet peculiarly. The methods employed in the persecutions in Denmark probably had a far greater and more cruel effect than those in any other country so far, because of the diabolic suddenness with which the nocturnal raid was launched. In the middle of the Hebrew New Year Festival, which also happened to be the Sabbath, when Jewish families normally gather together for the ceremony and when orthodox believers are forbidden by their religious code to avail themselves of any means of communication, the Gestapo and their helpers broke into Jewish homes. Fortunately, almost everybody had been warned in advance, thanks especially to a magnanimous German, Dr. Duckwitz, who is mentioned in Prime Minister Hans Hedtoft's introduction to this book. But many poor souls who had not heeded the warning to seek shelter outside their own homes were led away, all of them, the aged, the women, and even babies, under heavy curses and blows. They were thrown into the holds of German freighters waiting for that purpose in the Free Port of Copenhagen, and from thence were carried off to Germany.

Scenes beyond description took place during this

12

the Danish St. Bartholomew's and for a number of terrible days and nights afterwards. Several people committed suicide. We heard of fathers who killed their families and themselves to avoid a fate which they feared more than death. However, by far the majority found temporary places of refuge with non-Jewish countrymen, where they waited for an opportunity to escape. Along the beaches of Zealand other unhappy crowds were packed, hoping for a miracle, a Jewish Dunkirk which might free them from the hands of the barbarians. Some tried to row across on their own, using old, leaking boats. Many were drowned en route. Those who waited were nearly all of them saved by organizations of helpers which rapidly appeared.

On the other side of the Sound the Swedes were ready to receive the refugees. Immediately before the raid the Swedish government had made representations in Berlin to the effect that all Jews in Denmark should be allowed to emigrate to Sweden in a legal way so that the Germans could be freed from what they termed "the enemies of the people." Berlin never answered. But the offer remained in force: anybody who fled to Sweden would be received as a guest of the nation.

During the following months the biggest and most dramatic rescue action on either side of the Sound was carried through, quite unprecedented in Scandinavian history. It is about this that my little book

13

is going to tell you: what this event was like, as seen at close quarters by participants in the rescue work. The majority of the crossings were made from Zealand. It had to be so for the very simple reason that nearly all the Danish Jews lived in Copenhagen or its suburbs. But behind the transports there was the unanimous will of the Danish people. In those days it was welded together as never before, in mutual sorrow and exasperation.

The resistance was headed by old King Christian himself, the good friend and protector of the Jews. On an earlier occasion when the Germans brought pressure on the King and the government by threatening to introduce emergency laws under which the Jews, as in other countries, would have to carry the yellow Star of David, the King declared that he himself would be the first to carry it. The case was dropped. Both immediately before and after the raid the King sent a protest to Dr. Best. He was followed in this by the universities and the academies, which demonstrated by closing for some days, and by the Bishop of Zealand, who issued a pastoral letter containing a protest in the name of the Church and Christianity. It was read aloud in churches all over the country at the services the following Sunday, together with prayers for the persecuted Jews. Numerous protests from organizations of all kinds and demonstrations in the various districts of the country expressed the indignant contempt and aversion of

14

Danish men and women, old and young, yes, even of the children in the schools. As never before the Danish people faced the cruel countenance of Nazism in those days, and they will not easily forget what they saw.

In speaking of our reaction to the Nazi provocation of October 1943 there is one feature that should not be omitted: no assistance in the persecution of the Jews was offered the Gestapo by the German *Wehrmacht*. On the contrary, there is much evidence of the opposite. But it is a sad fact that some of the most eager persecutors of the Jews were our own Danish renegades and traitors. As in the accounts of all other Gestapo activities in Denmark during the war we constantly meet with names from the Danish *Hipokorps* (an abbreviation for the German word for auxiliary police forces). However, I believe that we may well term those cases exceptions which do not weaken the general impression of the events of those days in Denmark. We Danes as a whole can quite safely be proud of our contribution, in the face of history and the judgment of other nations.

Introduction

BY HANS HEDTOFT
PRIME MINISTER OF DENMARK

History will condemn the racialism and pogroms against the Jews as the most indelible stain on German Nazism. The swastika which the Nazis placed on Germany's flag will be remembered far into the future as the mark of barbarism, and it will spread the memory of the fall of a great nation under the vulgar philosophy of a mean, hysterical, and despotic Führer.
HARTVIG FRISCH, late Minister of Education, in *Denmark Occupied and Liberated.*

THE atrocities against the Danish Jews must never be forgotten, and every article helping to keep them fresh in our memories is valuable. Mr. A. Bertelsen's book is an honest contribution illustrating the attitude of the Danish people toward the persecution

16

of the Jews. At the same time it pleads eloquently against anti-Semitism.

During the fall of 1943 there had been frequent rumors that now the Germans were going to carry through a deportation of the Danish Jews similar to those already effected in other countries. However, just as frequently the rumors had been contradicted. Through most of the Occupation I had been in close contact with G. F. Duckwitz, who worked as an expert on shipping in the office of the German representatives in Copenhagen. Our conversations often centered round this problem, and Duckwitz had explained that all Germans in Denmark—probably except the Gestapo—were truly opposed to the pogroms and were going out of their way to prevent any such infamy in Denmark.

Toward the end of September, when nervousness was increasing in all quarters, Duckwitz pointed out to me that he feared that an end might be put to the current state of affairs, and on September 28, at a meeting in the old Workers' Assembly House in 22 Roemer Street, he looked me up. The disaster is here, he said. Everything is planned in detail. Ships will anchor in the roads off Copenhagen. Those of your poor Jewish countrymen who get caught by the Gestapo will forcibly be brought on board the ships and transported to an unknown fate. He was white with indignation and shame.

I admit frankly that—although through those

17

years I had been accustomed to receive many surprising pieces of information from this man—I was speechless with rage and fear . . . This was too devilish.

All I managed to say was, "Thanks for telling me," and Duckwitz disappeared. Personally he did everything that was humanly possible to save whatever lives could be saved. My friends Vilhelm Buhl, H. C. Hansen, Herman Dedichen, and I split up the different jobs between us. Through an illegal connection within the police forces we managed to have cars placed at our disposal, and off we went, each in a separate direction. I myself went first of all to the president of the Mosaic Religious Community, C. B. Henriques, an attorney, in one of the Copenhagen suburbs. I shall never forget my meeting with this man, the leader of the Danish Jews. We did not know one another very well, but we had met a few times. I believe that among other occasions I must have seen him during negotiations in the Employers' Union, for which Mr. Henriques was the legal adviser. I asked to see Mr. Henriques in private, and when we were alone I said, shaken, nervous, and unhappy as I was, "Mr. Henriques, a terrible disaster is going to take place. The action against the Jews, which we have feared, is about to be carried out. The procedure will be like this: on the night between the 1st and 2nd of October the Gestapo will raid all Jewish homes and then bring all Jews to ships in the harbor. You will have to warn every single Jew in this town immediately. It is obvious that we are ready to give you all the assistance we possibly can."

Today I can disclose that Mr. Henriques's reaction was quite different from what I had expected. He said only two words:

"You're lying."

And it took me a long time to convince him of my truthfulness.

"I do not understand how it can possibly be true," he repeated despairingly. "I have just returned from the Foreign Ministry, where I saw Director Svenningsen and he has reassured me. He said that he firmly believes that nothing will happen."

I answered that Mr. Svenningsen had made his statement in good faith. He could only report what the Germans said.

The following morning, September 29, there was an early morning service in the synagogue. It was the day of the Jewish New Year Festival, and on this occasion information of the imminent raid was given to the congregation.

I

Waiting for a Ship

Aт 5 A.M. on October 2, 1943, a small number of citizens from Lyngby gathered at the house of Mr. Boegh, the headmaster or principal of the school, in Ulrikkenborg Alle. The object of the meeting was to decide what could be done to help the Jews who had been living in our homes for some days. It was necessary to protect them from the imminent persecution. We did not even know whether the threat had become an established fact during that night, for rumor had it that the Germans had picked that very night for their raid because it was the Jewish New Year. Evidently they knew that believing Jews celebrate the great holy days among their relatives according to their old customs.

Present at the meeting were Mr. Frans Boegh, headmaster, and his wife and his son, Jorgen Boegh, Doctor of Divinity, who at that time worked on the *Christian Daily* and who therefore was better informed than the rest of us as far as many matters

20

were concerned. Then there were Mrs. Norrild, a lecturer's wife, from Sorgenfri, another Copenhagen suburb, and Miss Gregersen, a high school teacher from Buddinge Lane, a couple of our Jewish guests, and myself. The night before the head of the police at Lyngby, Chief of Police Mouridsen, had called on me and informed me that the police had observed concentrations of Gestapo forces with their so-called "prairie schooners" at the crossroads in the neighborhood. This might indicate that something conclusive was going to happen in the course of the night.

Jorgen Boegh thought that if there really was a raid it might be possible as early as the next day to obtain legal emigration permits for those Jews who had avoided capture. Despite the apparent improbability of this it was around this very conception that our hopes of rescuing the persecuted Jews were centered. Consequently, we agreed first of all to try to obtain a supply of visa forms, not only for "our own" Jews, but also for any others who might want our assistance to try this way out. The idea was to have all the forms duly filled in and gathered up, secretly and without exposing the Jews to any danger. Then the forms could be handed in collectively to the visa office the very minute permission to emigrate was given.

Recalling what happened that night and in the time that followed, it may appear a little strange that we could possibly base our work for the Jews on such a theory. But next day Mrs. Dora Berendsohn, who was married to my friend the German-Jewish professor Walter Berendsohn, confirmed that as a matter of fact there were many examples in Germany of emigration permits being granted Jews immediately after a raid. It is also likely that at that stage we were not ready to think of other than legal ways of helping the persecuted to escape Gestapo pursuit. We were soon to learn how absolutely mistaken we were that night, but I find it very interesting, and probably also characteristic, that it was on the basis of this mistake that the transport group from Lyngby grew up within a few days to comprise sixty members from this one suburban town and approximately the same number from Copenhagen and neighborhood.

At 6 A.M. I went to see the Chief of Police in his house on Buddinge Lane. He was shaving, and had just returned from the police station. It was almost superfluous to ask; his features clearly reflected what had happened. Two of his senior officers, he said, had just reported back from their duty on the coast, both of them greatly shocked by the horrors of the night. Many Jews had sought refuge in the bathhouses and boat sheds, and the officers had witnessed indescribable scenes when the Germans fell upon the Jews and dragged them off as prisoners, beating them and cursing them, hunting down and shooting at those who fled. The two police officers were not unaccustomed to roughness, but they would never, they said, never forget what they had seen, nor the cries of these wretched people.

I returned to the small group at Boegh's and told them what the chief had said. We promised each other that we would stand shoulder to shoulder to carry out the task we had undertaken, and then we parted.

I bicycled directly over to see Mr. Sigtryggson, the headmaster of my school, and told him what had happened in the course of the night. The German announcement in the early morning papers of the persecution confirmed my words—and I asked him if I could have a couple of days off from the school. The headmaster answered that naturally he fully sanctioned my intention to work for a cause which he, too, thought was far more important than anything else. All the same, to make sure that everything was in order I went straight down to Dr. Bondo, the district medical officer, and got a certificate of illness. I think we pretended that I had something wrong with my stomach.

My wife and I had already agreed that we would place ourselves as well as our house at the disposal of the work that now had to be done. Our children, too, Hans Peter 8, and Inger 10, were familiar with the situation. They had already made friends with our young guests, Ruth and Benjamin, and had become used to their strange orthodox customs at the table. They did not hesitate to take our advice to tell fibs to their friends in the neighborhood about their "cousins." Their indignation was unfeigned when one of their friends, who had perhaps caught a glimpse of our lodgers with their jet-black hair and strange features, allowed himself to express his doubt as to the relationship. There were to be many times when, for the sake of the cause we had decided to support, we had to deviate from the established moral code, but this was the only one when we were happy to realize that our children followed suit.

After the night of the raid a new and different situation was at hand. From now on the primary object was not merely to house and hide the two Jewish children, but also to help them to get out of the country, together with their parents and sisters and brothers, and all the rest of their friends of the same race, and their coreligionists. How this was going to be carried into practice was far from clear to us at that time, but both my wife and I probably realized that what was in waiting might bring about great changes in our lives.

Like many others in Denmark, I had found it hard to decide on my viewpoint during the political development of the Occupation. On April 9, 1940, I was employed as a teacher at a high school in Gävle in northern Sweden, so I watched the attack on my country from the outside, and I made the strange— and some may think unfortunate—observation that Denmark's freedom meant less to me than did the thought of home and my beloved ones. While I stood there in the teachers' room at Gävle reading mournfully but with horrified attention the telegrams about the doings of the German troops in Denmark, my thoughts circled round our semidetached house on Buddinge Lane, and I wished what I hardly dared face at that time, and what I dared not confess to others: I wished that my countrymen would surrender without fighting a hopeless fight, so that I could return to my country and find it, if not free, then still with my beloved ones safe and spared the devastations of war. Consequently, in all essentials I had been at first adherent of the so-called collaboration policy. My wife agreed to this. The events leading up to August 29, 1943, had, it is true, changed our views to some extent. We became members of an illegal organization called "Ringen," and usually we watched the increasing sabotage in Denmark with sympathy, although we could not help doubting whether we were justified in pursuing a course which seemed to be leading our country toward so-called "Norwegian conditions" of martial law.

So the dark night of the 1st and 2nd of October meant a personal dawn. From now on there was no doubt or uncertainty possible. In the face of these open acts of atrocity, insanely meaningless, it was not a question of one's viewpoint. Action was the word. Even under serious or desperate conditions it is often a happy feeling to be able to devote oneself to a cause that one feels convinced is both unconditionally just and absolutely binding. The situation in Denmark at that time was precisely that simple. No honest man could possibly refrain from action after this raid, when the persecuted cried for help. But how?

To get further details of the latest happenings I went down to the police station later that morning. Just as I entered the chief's office a young boy in his teens came in with some papers for endorsement. "Did you notice him?" asked Mouridsen when the boy had left. I remarked that he looked somewhat pale and ill. Mouridsen told me that his visit concerned a certificate of death. The boy's father, who was of Jewish descent, had suffered from heart disease, and yesterday he had had an attack as a result of the nervous excitement of the last months. In the night armed Gestapo men had knocked at his door. They demanded that he should get up and follow them. He answered that he was ill and unable to walk. "Then we'll drag you along!" they shouted. He then got up and put on his underwear, but fainted and fell across the bed. Having felt his pulse, they left him on the bed and led his wife and their three children away into a streetcar shed, where they were kept under guard for three hours before the wife managed to convince the Germans that she was no Jew. She and the children were then allowed to go home. When they got back home they found the father dead in the same attitude in which they had left him. One fate among many in those dark days.

When I asked the chief whether he thought that there was a chance the Jews might get an emigration permit within the near future, Mouridsen answered that he considered it very slight. However, it appeared that the staff at the visa office were of almost the opposite opinion. At any rate it was not improbable, they said, that it would be possible to issue emigration permits to Sweden, perhaps even the same afternoon.

We therefore sent for a great number of forms, and I took the majority back to Lyngby, but before I left I went down to the Ministry of Finance to see Mr. Dige, Permanent Undersecretary and a friend from my university years with whom I had remained in close personal contact. There I learned that Dr. Best had answered an application that day from the so-called "Government of the Permanent Undersecretaries" by stating that the raid would not be repeated. It was *"einmalig."* At that time I had not yet learned to understand the German jargon under the new regime. Otherwise I would have known that it meant: we shall hunt the Jews night and day in their homes, in the streets, in their hide-outs, on the coast, and on the sea on their way to safety, as long as there is one single one of them left in Denmark. At

27

that moment, however, Best's announcement almost seemed to me to support the hopeful suggestions from the visa office.

The rumor that visa forms could be had at Buddinge Lane spread like a forest fire. As early as Saturday afternoon our sitting room had to be converted into an office from which the Jews, through their friends or hosts, got the forms, and help to fill them in. In the course of the first couple of days we had about fifty ready to be handed in as soon as emigration to Sweden was opened.

In only one case did a Jew fetch the form in person. This daring exception was a female dentist who was hiding out with a family in Lyngby. She told us that the Germans and their Danish collaborators had called on her sister the night before. As the sister like herself was married to a non-Jew they had left her in peace; but they had taken away her eighty-four-year-old mother, who was completely deaf and unable to walk because of illness. The day before the raid her family had suggested that the mother should go to a hospital. As she did not like to leave home they had tried to explain to her that, being a Jew, she was in danger there but would be safe in a hospital. To this she had answered that surely the Germans would not bother to take her away. She was so decrepit that she did not realize that she could be dangerous to the Great German Reich! At any rate she was now being rendered harmless in the concentration camp of The-

28

resienstadt—if she had not died during the transportation.

We soon realized that we could not rest contented in the vague hope of obtaining legal permits for crossings to Sweden, and as early as Sunday, October 3, we succeeded in contacting an organization that arranged illegal transports. It was Mrs. Berendsohn who through one of our mutual German friends introduced me to Professor Richard Ege and his wife. When I called on them the following day I also met their assistants, Professor Brandt Rehberg and Professor Linderstrom-Lang, and a co-operation between the two groups, which should prove of great use to our joint objective, was arranged. I was happy because I had managed to get a contact to Sweden, but for the time being the routes of the Ege group were filled to capacity. For the first couple of days they could take only a very restricted number of passengers from Lyngby, and I therefore considered it necessary to be on the lookout for other means of transport as well.

The fact that so many people sought our assistance during the first week after the raid—about four or five hundred—is mainly due to David. Of the many unforgettable experiences of that stirring month, working together with him was one of the greatest. David is one of eight sisters and brothers in an orthodox Jewish family. In 1914 his father arrived in Sweden from Poland on his way to Russia, called up for the Russian army; in Malmoe, however, he was stopped by the Swedish authorities, and from there he had gone to Copenhagen where he had since made a living for himself and his family as a tailor and the owner of a shop dealing in second-hand clothes. He is a short, stout man with big brown eyes which sparkle with benevolence and inherent good humor, but tears, too, came easily into his eyes when he was moved. Like himself his wife had a typical Jewish appearance, a mild manner, and at the same time a strong nature. Both of them are anchored deeply in the rigorous East European Jewish orthodoxy, and at that time they and all their children belonged to the extreme orthodox synagogue in Ole Suhr Street.

David studied to become a veterinary surgeon, and after his return from exile in Sweden he passed his exam *cum laude,* and then took up the study of microbiology. And now, as this is being written, he lives in Israel and is employed by the state to set up bacteriological laboratories in the hospitals. As far as I know, his whole family is now in Israel.

David is learned as a rabbi in the laws of his people, and he keeps them conscientiously and rigidly. Others have told me that when on the Jewish New Year's Eve he phoned his coreligionists to prepare them for what was imminent, everybody realized the gravity of the situation. The holy tradition must not be broken unless for very urgent reasons, and the

30

very fact that of all persons David broke it by using the telephone proved that the danger must be incredibly imminent.

In a sense this young Jew was the actual founder of the relief action in Lyngby. A few days before the persecutions began he had appealed to the principal and the teachers of his old school, Christianshavn High School, and asked them whether they could possibly help him to hide a number of Jews who had no personal contacts outside Jewish circles. This was how Mr. Boegh, the headmaster, and Mr. Norrild, the lecturer, and their wives, provided some Jewish families with accommodations in Lyngby a week before the raid.

Incessantly, day and night literally, David was busy helping, completely disregarding his own dangerous situation. The Sunday following the raid he came to visit us for the first time—a happy meeting and a decisive moment in the history of the Lyngby Group. David had been called up as a police constable in the civil police force, and luckily he had kept his blue uniform and was therefore in a position to defy the curfew and walk in the streets after 8 P.M. He was on the go everywhere, and everywhere he looked up Jews and helped them out, always bubbling with activity, yet always well balanced, cheerful, but also cunning and levelheaded. When he slept —and that was usually only for a couple of hours —he spent the nights wherever it could be arranged,

31

most often on the divan in our sitting room with the door leading to the veranda ajar, in case there should be a visit by unwelcome strangers.

Quite unintentionally he was sometimes a bit troublesome as far as food was concerned. Even more than the other orthodox Jews I met at that time, David was bound by the rigorous dietary laws, and then he was always in a hurry. He did not touch our ordinary food, because what was made with butter, or milk, or lard was not *kosher* (clean) in a Jewish home, and meat of all kinds is prohibited unless the animal has been killed in conformity with the ritual killing methods, *schaechtning*. On top of this there were other difficulties as regards cooking and serving. Very soon my wife knew all about it, especially as she had already learned something about these problems from our two foster children. Unlike David, she did not believe that he could do without food, so she mixed him a sort of concentrated food, the main ingredients of which were egg yolks and claret, which satisfied even the most pious cookery book.

Apart from his meals David was extremely careful with himself. There was only one more exception: his shaving. For reasons unknown to me he allowed his black beard-stubble to grow unrestrained and vigorously. It gave his Jewish appearance an even more Hebrew touch. In the end I had to order him to shave, at the instigation of Professor Ege. The otherwise very levelheaded professor completely lost his balance when he saw the young Jew one day when we visited him at the institute and the atmosphere was very tense.

"Do you realize what you look like, young man? Your face is a danger both to yourself and your surroundings," he said.

Ege demanded that David should be sent to Sweden immediately. However, I could not agree to that. At that time we could still not do without him, and furthermore I knew that any attempt to persuade him to escape was doomed to fail, for he had decided that he would not leave Denmark until all Jews who needed his assistance had been brought to safety. On the other hand I had to concede to Professor Ege's point of view that it was absolutely irresponsible to let such a dark young man appear in public with that beard. So when we got back to Buddinge Lane I said to him,

"Now, look, David, get that beard off!"

"All right," said David, kind and obliging as always, "the only thing is that I shall have to go and get my razor first."

"Where?"

"In my apartment in Copenhagen."

"Under no circumstances! You will not leave this house until you have shaved!" Silence. "Now go into the bathroom and get that beard off. My razor is in there and everything else you may need."

33

David said, "Thank you so much, but unfortunately it is impossible."

"What do you mean?"

"I cannot use your razor."

"Why not? It is probably just as good as your own!"

David again insisted that he would go and get his own, this time with indications of stubbornness rather like one of the camels of his forefathers. But now my patience, too, was exhausted.

"What the dickens is the matter? What is wrong with my razor?"

"I am not allowed to use that sort of thing. Moses has directed that we must not shave the beard—only cut it. You can look it up yourself."

He even mentioned where I could find it in the Old Testament, I think, but I have forgotten just where.

"Nonsense! You are usually quite nicely shaved."

In the end he had to admit that he used an electric razor.

"For heaven's sake, then you do shave after all. Contrary to the Law!"

"No. An electric razor does not shave, it merely cuts the stubble."

At that time I had never seen an electric razor, and I felt that my offensive was breaking down. The technical experts were too strong for me. Cornered as I was, I had to resort to rather crude satire.

34

"It is really remarkable that Moses should have thought of electric razors as early as that."

I forget what David answered, probably nothing at all. Then all of a sudden I had a brain wave, one of those which are sometimes sent by heaven to people in decisive moments.

"O.K., let us suppose that according to the Law you must use an electric razor. But it says in the Talmud" (already my association with the believers had taught me a good deal about the Holy Scripture) "that if it is a matter of life and death—and that is exactly what it is here, both as regards you and all those who are still to be helped by you—it is permissible to disregard the commandments of the Law."

This proved a direct hit. David gave in instantaneously and went into the bathroom. Some time afterwards he appeared again at the top of the stairs. He was an unbelievable sight: his face was a symphony in white, black, and red. Here and there were clearings in the jungle. But there was blood on the white lather.

"I can't do it!"

His voice seemed to be between laughter and tears. The effect was indescribable. But the problem of David's beard still seemed far from solution. Then, just at the psychological moment, Mrs. Boegh rang the bell. She came like an angel from heaven: she knew a man in Lyngby who had an electric razor —probably the only one. Ten minutes later David again emerged from the bathroom, his face nicely cleared according to the precepts—and radiant. A few scratches still bore evidence of the horrors he had been exposed to. But as a matter of fact this was the only blood that was shed during the activities of the Lyngby Group.

I met David under circumstances where one soon learns to know the man behind the mask. Two months later we met again as refugees in Stockholm, both living with my wife's family. For a couple of weeks we had an opportunity to meet daily, and through a fruitful fellowship we could discuss the problems we both had deep in our minds. Here, too, I became acquainted with his constant, indefatigable endeavors through the Red Cross and other channels to bring help to the victims of the Nazi persecutions in the German concentration camps. David was a Jew right down to the root of his soul. He knew the Torah, the Pentateuch, better than most other people, and he submitted himself to its commandments in joyful and grateful obedience.

As a whole the usual Christian or Pauline conception of Jewish "slavery under the yoke of the Law" is a very misleading one. The relation between the good Jew and the Law is much better characterized, for instance, by the expression used in the Gospel according to St. Matthew (XI, 30) about the persecu-

36

tion of Christ: "My yoke is easy, and my burden is light." And to David—as well as to all other believing Jews, who understood it properly—the Law always was a means presented to them by the Lord to teach them self-control and Judaism's faith in God. In itself it was no goal at all. Consequently love for one's neighbor may make it imperative that exterior compliance with the letter of the Law should give way to the demands of life and the great commandment of altruism.

Like most of his coreligionists, David knew amazingly little about the greatest of all Jews and nothing about His Church. David had not been baptized. He was a good Jew, yet I consider him the best Christian —in the proper sense of the word—I ever met. As far as I am able to judge, he lived his life in the light of the double commandment, which to the Founder of Christianity as well as to His learned countryman was the basis of the Law: Thou shalt love the Lord thy God, and thy neighbor as thyself. (St. Mark XII, 28-34).

Sunday night we were visited by two young Jews on the run, one of them a German immigrant, the other David's younger sister, the "Queen Bee," as we called her, because she was qualifying herself for beekeeping so that one day she could go and settle down in Palestine. They had met one another by accident the same day and were now on their way to Elsinore where the man knew somebody who he thought might be able to smuggle them across to Sweden. The boat would leave at 9 P.M., he said, and it was now 7:30. There was no train for Elsinore after that time, and cars were not allowed to drive long distances under the occupation. Exempted were only doctors' cars. So I phoned Dr. Bondo, the district medical officer, and asked him to come immediately: My daughter Inger was ill in bed with a temperature of 104, and we feared that it might be appendicitis—all is fair in war and under persecution. Dr. Bondo was there almost immediately, and he grasped the situation equally quickly. He would very much like to help, but it would be much too dangerous for the Jews to go with him in his car, as Elsinore was outside the permitted thirty-kilometer zone. There was probably some chance of getting an ambulance, but the hour was so late that it would be impossible to get up there in time to catch the boat. All the same, later on that evening the two refugees started off by train in the direction of Elsinore, hoping that in the course of the night some further means of transport might show up. The following day the Queen Bee phoned me. There had been no passage available from Elsinore, so she had gone on to Humlebæk, and she said that she felt sure that the boat that was going to take her across that night could hold about fifty of "our" Jews as well.

We thought we ought to try this chance, so we set

about preparations for the departure at once. My wife phoned to the various homes where Jews were staying. I myself went off to pick up an elderly married couple. Orders as to luggage were to the effect that for the crossing only as much was allowed as could be carried in a small bag or briefcase. The two old people, however, thought that they could not do with less than two heavy trunks and one carpetbag. There was not much time for discussion, and when on our way to the station I demanded that the lady should put all she really needed in one trunk and leave the other one behind she burst into tears, and her complaints did not stop until I had promised that I would look after the rest of the luggage myself and guarantee that it would be carefully stored. It proved difficult to keep the promise, but as a matter of fact I had the trunk along with me all through the day and the night, and later on, when I met the two old people in Sweden, I could set their minds at rest by telling them that their property was absolutely safe, and that they could pick it up on their return.

On our arrival at the railroad station at the very last minute I discovered much to my alarm that none of the other cars had arrived as arranged. Nor did we see any of the Jews from Copenhagen who were under our protection. But I took comfort in the thought that in all probability they had driven right up to Humlebæk in spite of the fact that Humlebæk was outside the permitted zone. However, we did not meet them there either, and nobody knew anything about any cars from Lyngby or Copenhagen. At Humlebæk I felt for the first time the crushing mixture of irresolute despair and consciousness of guilt which I met so often later on, along with the feeling that I had taken upon myself a responsibility far beyond all common sense and my own qualifications. Where were all the rest? Hadn't they been able to get away? Or had they turned back, perhaps? Or, worst of all, had they been caught by the Germans on their way up here?

As for ourselves, there was nothing to do but to take cover in some houses pointed out to us near the station. Here, at 2 Station Avenue, we were received with great hospitality by our excellent hosts, Mr. Petersen, his wife, and their grown-up son. All the rooms, both upstairs and downstairs, were already crammed with refugee Jews when we arrived. But there was no one there from our group.

Driven by a gnawing uneasiness, I went back again immediately to the station to look for those we had lost. As I neared the building I saw a single band of Jews with their leaders. Each of them carried a well-known Copenhagen afternoon paper in his hand: the mark of identification we had agreed upon. They, too, were taken down to the Petersens' in Station Avenue. But where was Prior, my colleague from the State High School, and his charges, the Katzenstein family with their many children?

And where was Miss Kaer with her Jewish brother-in-law and his family? Suddenly I saw her coming out from behind the station building, and a little later I was hailed by Prior, who like the others had driven there directly by car. Boisterous joy on both sides followed. I felt like embracing them all—and I probably did.

It was the second time Miss Kaer made me lose my balance. The first time was for quite a different reason, and in another way. I shall mention that short episode as an example of how strained our nerves were, and how suspicion was on guard in those days.

A young Jew who was hiding with a Miss Ulff, who was then a domestic science teacher at Lyngby, had given me a couple of addresses in another Copenhagen suburb. There, I was told, it should be possible for me to get some information about his parents and other relatives who were trying to obtain contacts to get across to Sweden, but in vain. He also gave me the name and address of his brother's fiancée Miss Kaer, who was not a Jew. She worked with her fiancé's family in a tailor shop in Copenhagen.

After some difficulty I found the shop and asked to see Miss Kaer. The shop assistant behind the counter answered abruptly that she was not in. He would not say anything about the family, the owners of the shop, and he pretended that he knew nothing

41

about a connection between Miss Kaer and the family. On the whole, he was extremely disagreeable and obviously lacking in brains. I then wrote a short message to the young girl suggesting that she phone me, and she did so in the afternoon. I asked her to come to Buddinge Lane to discuss a matter of importance to her family, but she answered in a chilly manner that she could not see that we had anything to discuss. As I declared that it was absolutely imperative that she should come, she finished our brief conversation in a voice that sent a chill of hostile suspicion through the telephone: "I don't understand it all, but I'll think it over. I may come around 6 o'clock."

She arrived at the time stated, and I was surprised by the striking contrast between the light blond, pretty young girl and the strangely hard, almost petrified expression in her face. I started by explaining why I had approached her, and I mentioned what I had learned about her brother-in-law. In the end I asked her to tell what she knew about her fiancé's whereabouts, and where his family might be. Instead of answering she shouted, her voice trembling with excitement.

"What do you want? What's behind this conversation? There's not one thing in all you have said that's true. Nothing!"

From what had already happened I had not anticipated a pleasant conversation, but this was a bit too much of a good thing. And it became worse!

42

"You say that you want to help us. But I don't believe that you mean any good to the man you are talking about, or his family!"

I felt more and more overwhelmed, perhaps by her tone rather than by the accusation behind her words, but I still tried to control myself and my smoldering anger.

"I hardly think that we understand one another," I said. "Tell me plainly, what do you think I am?"

"I don't know. But if you knew what I have been through the last few days you would understand why I have no confidence in you."

Now I, too, lost my head, and shouted just as hot-headedly, "Well, and what then? Do you mean to say that I am an informer—or what?"

"I know nothing at all! I only know that what you have told me cannot be true, and I don't trust you!"

Despite my excitement I must have understood that convincing facts were needed more than words, for I went up to the door and opened it, and going into the dining room I said—not very politely, I am afraid—"Come in here!"

As we entered the room Benjamin and Ruth came toward me. I embraced Benjamin and, patting his cheeks under the chequered Jewish skullcap, I said, "Look at these faces. Do you really believe that they would be here if I were what you think I am?"

The young girl's suspicious attitude started relaxing and suddenly she burst into tears.

43

"I was wrong about you. Now I don't know what to think. Can you tell me anything more?"

"Do you know the bazaar at Enghave?" I asked.

The young girl jumped up with an exclamation of joy. "Yes, that's right!"

"And 15 Enghave Lane, 5th floor?" I continued. Those were the addresses her brother-in-law had given me besides her own.

"That's right, all of it. Thank God. But you have got one thing wrong. The young man you mentioned is not where you said he was."

She was not exactly the easy type to convince. I had met the young man at Miss Ulff's that very same afternoon! But now, remembering a line from a play, "It's an awkward matter, Sir, to argue with women-folk, particularly when they are madly in love," I started again.

"If I lead you to him and let you see him in person, face to face, will you be convinced then?"

"I probably will, but you can't do it."

Off we went to see Miss Ulff—but on the way down there we made a detour to deliver a message to the two Katzensteiners who lived with the Dragsted family in Engelsborg Road—and then we went straight up to the room in the attic where we had agreed that the young man should hide. He was not there!

"You see, it's just as I said, I told you so," said

Miss Kaer in a tone in which I recognized an under-current of the suspicion she had just overcome.

The very same moment he came up from one of the rooms below. Happy reunion, indeed! I think that I myself felt almost as relieved as the young couple. Of all the things we experienced during the trans-ports, the suspicion among the people we considered ourselves called upon to help that we might betray them was one of the things that made the greatest impression on me.

A couple of nights later I put the young man and his parents on the boat, without suspecting that shortly afterwards we should meet again on the other side of the Sound under happier circumstances. It happened in Malmoe a few months later when I served as best man at his wedding in the synagogue. The very fact that I was invited to attend such a sig-nificant ceremony as a wedding is certainly an unu-sual proof of friendship toward a nonbeliever, but when, after the ceremony in the synagogue, we all gathered for the reception the bridegroom and his parents came up to me in a way I shall never forget. The stout old man threw his arms around my neck and kissed both my cheeks, saying something I did not understand. Then he buried his face in his hands and burst into tears.

I do not know whether Jews feel more intensely than we do, but I have often been impressed at how strongly and spontaneously they express their gratitude. Now, more than eight years afterwards, I cannot help feeling happy at the constantly repeated proofs from Jewish friends that they, too, have not forgotten what happened then.

So gradually now the houses round the station became crowded with people waiting for the ship. To our great disappointment it turned out to be impossible to get into contact that night with any skippers. Nobody knew anything of the boat which was supposed to be able to hold all our Jews from Lyngby, and for whose sake we had moved up here. As a whole very little seemed to have been done in Elsinore to organize aid for the refugees. However, even on the first night we were convinced that one thing that was not lacking was good will, a fact which was proved by the very house we stayed in. Every square inch of the floor was filled to capacity, a significant piece of evidence. And our experiences during the following days made it clear that there were many more kind hosts like Petersen in Station Avenue.

II

Thoughts in a Hayloft

LATE that night there was a telephone message that the Gestapo was searching the houses along the coast, so we felt it necessary to leave the house and move into the country. The weather was very unpleasant, with strong winds, heavy rain, and pitch darkness. The goal of our wanderings was a farm two or three miles inland, sufficiently far away from the high road. We went into the stable, and from there up a narrow ladder to the loft, where we were allowed to sleep in the straw. On our way to the farm a few elderly and feeble Jews and a woman in an advanced stage of pregnancy had been put up for the night in a nearby house. The rest of us made ourselves as comfortable as possible in our loft.

We were about fifty in all. Here as so often later on I had a good opportunity to admire the calmness with which the Jews endured their lot. A baby cried for a short while; otherwise there was no indication of nervousness, let alone despair. I did not understand how it was possible for people to sleep under these circumstances, but the Jews soon fell asleep, apparently as confident and peaceful as children.

It is possible that a fatalistic inclination, acquired in the course of millenniums of experiences of this kind, has become an essential quality in the Jew. In the days before the raid we were often amazed to notice in Lyngby how carelessly, even improvidently, in a manner bordering on irresponsibility, they acted under serious conditions. Take, for instance, some of those who were now sleeping in the loft. Once when they became bored at being cooped up indoors against their will, they went out, walked down the street in one big crowd, and took up their stand opposite Sorgenfri, the Royal Palace. There they stood watching with great interest the German sentries outside the palace—even while they themselves were being watched equally intensely by a Danish Nazi who lived in the same street as they did. They did not understand it when their hosts reproached them because of their carelessness and even less when the same day they were moved to a different part of the town.

But that night in the hayloft I did not feel anything but admiration for their quiet and resigned submission to fate—admiration, even with a certain amount of envy, based on a sense of inferiority to these unfortunate children of a people in persecution, consecrated to suffering, and threatened by destruction.

48

For while I was lying there, listening to the quiet breathing of these Jews as they slept, I felt that among them they had a treasure whose value was immeasurable for us, the existence of which they perhaps did not even realize themselves. Theirs was community in faith, and a solidarity in hope inherited from their Old Testament ancestors throughout their bloodstained history. These things have given them a sense of confidence amid all the vicissitudes of life. This feeling of belonging to the joint *bet abot*, the house of their fathers, the great family of the chosen people, is the firm essence of Judaism, and of the soul of the individual Jew.

I knew very well that there were religious differences between the orthodox Jews and the rest, and class barriers and classifications between the rich and the poor, and later on I learned that even among the orthodox Jews the art of carrying a knife in one's sleeve is not unknown. But through all I went through then and later with the nonassimilated Jews, during those dark days and nights on the coast, in my everyday life with the children and the young Jews in the refugee school in Sweden, at the sabbaths in the families and in the synagogue, in the orthodox camp at Helsjoen near Gothenburg, where I stayed for some days among the most pious of the pious (there were several hundred of them)—I noticed with astonishment and respect their complete unity on all the essentials. This has preserved the Jewish people during its almost two thousand years of exile.

I understand very well the strange, and to detached spectators the frequently unpleasant, absurdity of the orthodox *kosher* regulations, but I shall not forget—because I have witnessed it—that to all these people all this is a sacred tradition. In effect it coins the precious treasures from their religion, from the scriptures and their religious services, into the small change of everyday life. Consequently, at the same time it establishes the connection between heaven and earth, and makes the community among the believers a reality for every hour of the day.

The crowd in the hayloft in Humlebæk was made up of comparatively few, but large families. They all come back vividly to my mental eye. I have kept in touch with several of them, and I hope that nobody will mind if I take this opportunity to mention some of their names, and to tell something of their stories.

Here, for instance, was Mr. Katzenstein, sleeping. He was a Danish-born teacher of Hebrew in Hamburg, Germany, before the war. He lay there surrounded by his wife and most of their children. They had a fine brood of fourteen. There was Ella with her beautiful, radiant eyes and her lively face, quiet Ruth, and Raphael and Benjamin with their jet-black hair, and many others. No wonder that the father was proud, both of the size of his family and of its quality. The first night I visited him in Lyngby at Prior's, where he lived with one of the boys, he confided to me that 1924 was the memorable year of his marriage, for "that year we had no babies."

That same Friday afternoon Mr. Meier, who was also sleeping in the loft with his family, introduced me for the first time outside my reading to the orthodox laws. Mr. Meier was staying with a family at Nybro Road, and when I entered his home he was sitting in a darkened room with an unlit cigar between his fingers.

"Will you be kind enough to light my cigar, please," he said. Of course I did. "I am not allowed to do it myself, you see," he added as an explanation.

I did not really understand.

"Well, you see," he told me, "we are now celebrating our Jewish New Year, and we are not supposed to make a light during a holiday."

I thought I had heard that before. "But it is all right for *me* to light the cigar, I suppose, and then when it has been lit you are allowed to smoke it?" I asked.

"Yes, certainly. For the same reason I must ask you to switch on the light if you do not prefer to sit in the darkness."

After a pleasant conversation, during which I learned a lot about the Jewish religion which was new and surprising to me, I said good-by to him, and also to nine-year-old Abraham, who had been sitting in the next room enjoying the unusual holiday

51

light. As I was leaving I asked Mr. Meier, "What would have happened if you had forgotten that it was the Sabbath and by accident you had lit your cigar yourself? What would you have felt?"

"Then I would have felt in my conscience that I had committed a great sin because I had violated the Lord's commandment to my people. And will you kindly remember, please, to switch the light off in the hall when you leave—and in Abraham's room as well. I don't know if Mr. Nielsen will return to-night, and it would be absurd to leave the light on during the whole night for no reason."

Mr. Meier and his family belonged to a most scrupulous and law-abiding group among the believers, I am sure, but full orthodoxy is not really proved by this example. In Sweden I once spent the Sabbath with a Danish Jewish family, and there I experienced something which showed to me that there are degrees of piousness, and that others adhere to a more rigid interpretation of the prohibitions of the Mosaic Law against making fire during the Sabbath.

I had been asked to arrive before the hour when the Sabbath begins, and at once the family asked me to do them the favor of putting out the light in the adjoining rooms when I left after the festival, but would I please leave it on in the hall.

I wondered a bit why they considered it necessary to instruct me *prior* to the festival of what I should do *after* it, but I soon understood that it must be linked up with a more rigorous compliance with the law than I had met before. When we sat down at the table the master of the house asked me kindly, but a little shyly, to put my hat on during the meal. In other families I had been considered a guest at the Sabbath without any obligation to comply with the regulations, which, of course, meant nothing to a non-Jew. Naturally I did not mind covering my head with a felt hat, as unlike my Jewish male friends I did not have a skull cap. I also abstained from smoking, since one was not supposed to make fire on the Sabbath. But what embarrassed me a little was that I could not help feeling that the husband and wife disagreed considerably with regard to the religious laws, and when the discussion became hot they appealed to me as a kind of umpire—a flattering, but heavy responsibility to place on the shoulders of a poor *shabbas goi* whose sole duties were limited to the performance of those things which piety prohibits the believers to do themselves on the Sabbath.

I do not remember the details, only that in most cases my judgment was in favor of the less pious of the parties, the wife. Incidentally, this was the only occasion among Jewish friends when I was not completely touched and absorbed by the strange, mixed atmosphere of the religious festival, the home atmosphere, and a certain spirit of gaiety, which are the blessings of the Sabbath for the believers.

When I left I had forgotten about my promise. I

noticed that when I said good-by the host looked at me in a strange, urgent way, but as he did not say anything I opened the door and went out into the hall.

He ran up to me, seized me by the arm, and started uttering strange sounds, something like, "Umm, umm, umm!"

I probably looked a bit confused. At any rate the hostess considered it necessary to explain her husband's behavior.

"Well, sir, it is a little difficult when a man is so pious that he isn't even allowed to ask you to switch off the light," she said.

I turned off the light quickly—but in the hall.

"Um, um, um," and the big man was buzzing round me again like a bumblebee, flapping his wing-cases toward the sitting room: that was where I should have put out the light. Then, finally, I took the hint and fulfilled my obligations toward the family's electricity bill.

I quote these personal experiences with the characteristics of orthodox Judaism although I am fully aware that among non-Jews they may cause amazement and perhaps distaste, just as in my time I myself met them with surprise. It is not everybody who can understand that it is inevitable that the Jews must be allowed to be different as regards their creed and religious customs and traditions, and that a people who for two and a half millenniums has taken strength and consolation from the words of the Law must have the same right as adherents of other religions to have divergent opinions as to the interpretation and fulfilment of their holy scriptures. Criticism in this respect from Christian quarters can reasonably be met with references to the fact that within Christianity there are many diverging dogmas and religious traditions, which constitute barriers between the religious communities. And, by the way, how is our own religion viewed from outside?

One night I discussed these questions with a good friend of mine who was of Jewish descent but as far as I know without any great personal interest in religion. She told me that recently she had attended a religious service with communion in a Danish established church. "You cannot imagine my surprise when I heard the vicar say, handing out the bread and the wine, 'This is the body of Jesus Christ, and this is the blood of Jesus Christ.' I couldn't believe my own ears! He told them to eat Jesus like meat and blood! As far as I know the Lord's Supper is an essential part of the Christian faith. But may I ask you: can you mention any tenet of orthodox Judaism which would seem as absurd as this to an outsider?" I still have no answer ready for this question.

Of all the Jews in the loft in Humlebæk, the one who made the deepest impression on me was old Fuchs. I can still see this nearly eighty-year-old man before me as he climbed the ladder to the loft, erect and without any difficulty. He was short, square-built, stout, like a man in his best years, with almost no wrinkles, a clear complexion, and mild calm eyes. His white beard shone in the scanty light from the stable lantern. Fuchs was a *Schaechter* by trade, that is, the butcher of his congregation. He had received his training for this at Jewish schools in Poland, and he was highly respected because of his rectitude and learning. When he sat down to narrate legends from the Talmud, or interpreted the Law, all the others squatted around him, their eyes radiant, and in such moments they were evidently able to forget everything else around them.

Thinking back at these scenes in the loft, I understand the spirit that is still living in the Jewish people of today, the spirit which was expressed so proudly by the woman from Shunem when she refused the offer made by Elisha the prophet to reward her with royal favor and presents: "I dwell among mine own people." (II. Kings IV, 13.) What more did she need?

Among my Jewish friends were also David's parents and his brothers and sisters. Along with the other members of the Danish family who lived in this country they were the last survivors of a large family. About two hundred of its members, all of them from the father's side, had ended their lives in the German gas-chambers in Poland. Now they were sleeping

56

here with a threat of the same fate over their heads, confident among their own people.

However, I could not sleep, I was haunted by painful thoughts. What would be the result of all this? What right had we to defend the lives of these people? Nothing but the best intentions—just like thousands of other Danes, otherwise nothing—and at any rate far less possibility of helping, than numerous others who knew the surrounding country and had practical knowledge of this kind of work. We knew almost nothing about the neighborhood, and even less about the population, and we had no contacts among the fishermen who were to help us. I was lying there gazing up through the cracks in the roof and into pitch-black, empty darkness. I tried to keep my lower jaw steady. It annoyed me that my teeth chattered so that they probably disturbed those sleeping around me. On our way from the house in Station Avenue I had fallen headlong into a deep ditch and had been soaked through by muddy water, and now I was lying on the bare floor covered only with my raincoat. A young colleague lying behind me must have heard me—he could not have seen me—and now he covered me carefully with some straw. It did not help much. Good intentions, and a sort of teeth-chattering responsibility—that was all we had. And the blind confidence of the Jews, of course. It must have been blind since they did not see how little we commanded. Imagine, if things happened the way my despair made me see it: that the Jews were caught because of our weakness. I dared not finish my train of thought. . . . And then, on the other hand, somebody had to take over the leadership and the responsibility. And for some reason or other it had accidentally—or was it fate?—fallen to our lot. Good or not good: there was no other human possibility than to do the best we could, and then hope that we should be successful in spite of everything, in spite of ourselves! For the time being it must be considered a good omen that we had managed to get up here to this loft without mishap. It was obvious that the Germans had been neither very eager nor—at any rate -very thorough or clever as regards the raid, since there was no guard at the station. Even a single Gestapo man or informer could have made an enormous haul.

My nocturnal reflections in the loft were interrupted only by the homely sounds of the horses in the stable below, or when one of the guests in the loft turned round in the straw. A couple of times one of our colleagues brought in a message from the coast, but every time it was negative: there could not be any crossing that night.

At five in the morning I left the farm to catch the early train to Copenhagen.

III

Problems of Finance

Wʜᴇɴ I left the loft at Humlebæk it was obvious to me that our work had now entered a new and decisive phase. The people we had brought to Humlebæk must be helped to get away from there, and we were responsible for that even if it should prove necessary for us to take the initiative and organize the transportation ourselves. It would even be preferable to do this for all those who had already registered with our "office" at Lyngby, and for those who were looking for a chance to get across from there without having contacted us.

But in order to succeed in doing so it would be necessary to concentrate on three objectives: We had to find fishermen and skippers who could and would undertake crossings on a large scale. Money to pay for those who could not pay for their crossings must be provided. Finally, we should have to try to find a far larger number of active helpers both at Humlebæk and at Lyngby.

59

So far I did not know how all this should be done, but I felt that I could make myself much more useful in Lyngby and Copenhagen, where I had my connections, than at the actual scene of operations on the coast. Younger people and people who knew more about the surroundings, had better take the lead there. Among the helpers of Jews I had met at Humlebæk on my arrival, I had especially attached myself to a young man who had gone up there a couple of days earlier to help his married sister's Jewish family. He seemed to be well acquainted with the neighborhood, and from the very first moment he struck me as a man worthy of the utmost trust. Before I left the loft, I woke him, and in the faint light from his flashlight I gave him the money I had collected. This amounted to 13,000 kroner (at that time the rate of exchange was 20 cents to 1 krone), and asked him to use it if during the day it should become possible to arrange a crossing.

People may think that this was a reckless way of handling so much money, but my only answer must be that it could not be helped. Only under such conditions can that kind of work be done. The entire economy of the assistance to the Jews could be based on nothing but a personal relationship of trust. Money was paid and received without the giving of any receipts at all, to say nothing of any kind of account-keeping. It was imperative that nothing be written down which might get into the hands of the Germans.

Very frequently it has been said that the fishermen and skippers who sailed the Jews across charged too much for transportation. Several thousand kroner per passenger has been quoted as their price, though everybody considered it a matter of course that the helpers ashore worked without getting any kind of payment. Very often their contribution has been emphasized at the expense of that of the sailors. Without defending what actually happened in regard to exorbitant prices in certain cases I find it necessary to stress here that it was universally recognized among the helpers of the Jews that those who actually manned the boats deserved good pay for their work. They risked considerably more than all the others. If they got caught they stood to lose their means of subsistence, their boat or ship, to say nothing of being in direct danger of their lives. These conditions were definitely connected with that kind of work. I remember from some negotiations one day in October that a young fisherman, who had sailed for us a couple of times but who later refused to participate any more, answered my question as to why he had given up trying to help these unfortunate people by saying that he had promised his wife not to go on taking such risks, although it had been more profitable than his normal work. His wife's nerves could not stand it any more. The last time he had been out there had been exchanges of shots between the Gestapo and some saboteurs among the Jews on board. When I suggested that in the future we should send the saboteurs across via special routes he agreed to resume the work.

The principal rule of the financing of the transports had to be, of course, that the Jews paid for themselves and also helped those of their fellow sufferers who had not enough money. But as early as the first night it had appeared that there were many poor people, and comparatively few who could afford to pay anything much for the others. It cannot be denied that in a few individual cases the will to pay was lacking. I remember one example.

After the Liberation when I returned from my exile in Sweden I found a savings-bank book in my desk marked with a number and with a deposit of 1,000 kroner. I phoned the savings bank and asked the manager to take the book and return it to the owner. I pointed out to him that it had no doubt come into my possession as payment for a transport. The manager confirmed the correctness of my suspicion. He gave me the name of the Jew in question, and then told me the latter's story of his case. He had gotten on board the ship after paying the 500 kroner which was the price of the crossing, but somewhere off the shore the skipper stopped the boat and demanded that those on board who had already paid should pay him the rest of their money and securities. Otherwise he would turn round and sail them back again. So the unfortunate man had had to hand over his last means in the shape of his savings-bank book.

Having heard this statement I maintained that it could not possibly be correct, for how, then, would he explain the fact that now the book was in my desk if the grasping skipper had "blackmailed" him in the middle of the Sound. It did not take long to clean up the case. The same morning I had a visitor, Bjarne Sigtryggsson, the leader of the group which undertook the crossings from Humlebæk. I told him what I had heard. Sig remembered the real facts of the case. It was on one of the first days of the transports. The boat was ready to leave, the price was 500 kroner per person. As usual it appeared that some of the Jews had not got so much money, so Sig suggested that those who had money left should help the others. However, the funds raised in this way did not suffice, so he had to ask for help a second time. One of the Jews then drew his attention to the man with the savings-bank book. When asked to hand over the book for the benefit of his fellow sufferers he declared that he had paid for his ticket with 500 kroner, and that he did not intend to contribute more than that. Then Sig took out 500 kroner and handed it to him saying, "Here you are. Here is your money back. The car is still waiting and can take you back to where you came from."

The method proved effective. The man handed him the book immediately. You may call it a sort of blackmail, which was later on converted into a kind of compulsory saving, as I handed over the book to the savings bank. The story may serve not only as an example of the line of action which we then considered necessary and justified under the circumstances, but also as a warning against trusting uncritically the rather numerous stories which were told about ruthless exploitation by the skippers of their defenseless victims among the passengers.

The economic aspect of the history of the Jew Transports was not the least remarkable one. From the vicar of Lyngby, Pastor Krohn, I received on my return from Humlebæk an offer to raise a fund to help us. At the same time he brought me a lot of certificates of baptism, signed by the vicar and furnished with the seal of the Church but otherwise blank, which I might use at my own discretion in cases where it was suitable to be able to present a non-Jewish name—one of the many examples which prove how in those days we moved in a world beyond the usual conceptions of law and righteousness with the most matter-of-course feeling, though under normal conditions such a transaction would have seemed more than shocking.

I received with thanks both his offer and the certificates. On his rounds through the parish Pastor

Krohn also visited Mr. Johannes Fog, a timber merchant, and asked for an amount to help Mr. Bertelsen's transports.

"Mr. Bertelsen? Who is he?" asked the timber merchant.

When Krohn had told him what he knew about the person and the cause, Mr. Fog gave him 2,000 kroner and added, "Tell him that I'm willing to grant him a loan of another 10,000 kroner." And as the vicar was leaving the office he shouted, "Tell him I'll make it 20,000."

In the following few days the number of crossings increased rapidly. Soon the 20,000 was spent. But Fog was good for more. Within ten days I had borrowed 148,000 kroner from him on top of the 20,000.

On the night of one of our big transports he brought the money himself, as usual bicycling through a pouring rain.

"You are certainly an exacting creditor," he said when I met him on the steps, "You force an old man like me to get out late in the evening in this rotten weather! First I had to rush from my home to the bank manager's. He was not at home. I found him at a party a hell of a long way off. Then we biked to the bank cashier's place—there must be two of the bank employees present whenever large sums are paid out in cash—and then down to the safe. Here's the money. You asked for 20,000, but I know you by now, so for the sake of convenience I brought 30,000."

"Well, thank you very much," I answered, "I think I can manage to spend it all. But, you know, this is gradually amounting to quite a lot of money, and you probably realize that I have nothing besides my pay at the school. I can only hope that we shall find a solution for this, if not before, then when the Germans have left this country. And if others won't pay, then I guess the Danish state will have to do so."

"I certainly hope so," said Mr. Fog, and laughed heartily. "Otherwise the future does not appear to be too rosy for me."

As far as I know Mr. Fog is, and probably was, a well-to-do man, but all the same he had to get the money from the bank by raising a loan. The 148,000 kroner was no trifle to him either.

Fortunately, it did not prove necessary to apply to the state—I am afraid we might not have been successful just then. However, less then ten days after the loan had been raised I had repaid every bit of it, and at the same time the transports were kept going and demanded constant and considerable amounts.

The money arrived through strange channels—and secret ones at that time. One day Mr. Skat Roerdam, head of a department in the Ministry for Commerce, called on me. Shortly before that we had had quite a heated argument in his villa in a Copenhagen suburb while we were discussing the organization of the transports; however, we separated in all friendliness. I thought that he had come to continue the discussion, but I was wrong. Out of his pocket Mr. Skat Roerdam pulled a packet wrapped in brown paper. "I have heard that you owe Mr. Fog some money," he said. "Here's an instalment." The packet contained 70,000 kroner, one hundred forty 500-kroner notes.

Perhaps this is the right place to correct a misunderstanding in Dr. Jorgen Gersfelt's very sympathetic reference to the activities of the Lyngby Group in his book: *How We Fooled the Gestapo*. When he refers to me as a man "who had no other income than his salary from the school," and who then, if he had attempted to repay a personal debt of 150,000 kroner, "would have had to labor and suffer the rest of his life," then he is only too right—God help me! But the thought that I personally was liable for this large amount never really occurred to Mr. Fog or to me. He took the whole risk on his shoulders. That is also the reason I am glad to dedicate this narrative to Mr. Fog. His contribution was decisive in a critical period. But to pour money out, even for the best purpose, is a prosaic and dull business. It was we, the others, who had all the experiences, all the excitement—and I nearly said: all the fun. He deserves a great part of the honor, if anyone does.

It is a bit strange to think back at people and their

67

attitude toward money in those peculiar times. One morning on my way back from Humlebæk after a nightly transport had been sent off I was standing in the aisle of the subway train from Klampenborg with David and Prior. We were talking about what was on our minds, and we did it as quietly as one usually discusses that sort of thing. It was inconceivable that anybody could overhear our conversation. Yet suddenly a woman in the car got up from her seat and went straight up to me and said, "Would you like some money?"

"Yes, thank you, very much," I said immediately. She took her purse out of her bag and emptied its entire contents in bills into my hand, and then went back again to her seat without further comment. I do not remember having seen her before or after that.

That minor incident is one of many which proves that the thought of what was going on along the Danish coasts, and the will to help the persecuted, penetrated the entire atmosphere of our country then. Money poured in from all quarters, for instance, from schools where the pupils made their contributions toward the transports. But it takes a considerable time to collect 1,000 kroner if the money has to come from one hundred different sources, and here more than anywhere else the saying that quick help is double help held good.

My first thought when the registration with us of destitute Jews began to increase was that I would go direct to the government, which then existed under the Germans only in the shape of a management by the heads of individual departments, in this particular case represented by a single person, Mr. Dige of the Ministry for Finance. I did so quite confidently, feeling convinced that if it was humanly possible he would help. As I had expected, I met the most complete understanding when I explained my reasons for coming to him, but I soon realized that direct help from the Treasury was inconceivable. If the Germans got the slightest suspicion that the state was granting funds for purposes directly contrary to German interests, it might bring about the most serious consequences for the entire Danish people. At that time the German control of our finances was so thorough that it would have been extremely difficult to camouflage any payments to assist the Jews. On the other hand, we both considered it an absolutely intolerable thought that the Danish state had had to pay a fine of 1,000,000 kroner for a German who had been killed during some disturbances not long ago, while now many persecuted Jews were in danger—if the necessary means were not provided—of being handed over to a fate which everybody considered worse than death.

Without any definite promise from Mr. Dige—except that he would do his best to find a way out—I left him with a hope amounting almost to certainty that the economic problem of the help to the Jews would eventually be solved. And I was not disappointed! Not only did private individuals, men like Mr. Fog, devote great sums to the relief work, but other sources as well soon supplied us with ample means to carry it on.

One obvious solution was to ask for help from Jewish capital itself. Prompted by David, I called on a man, a non-Jew, who was in close contact with the Jews. We knew that he must have some knowledge about a relief fund—supposedly a rich one—belonging to the Mosaic Religious Community. This excellent man expressed his deepest sympathy with the poor unhappy refugees. He himself was toiling night and day to help, he said, but when we touched on the question of money, he declared that in any case the fund in question could not be touched. The money was in a trust fund for certain definite purposes, and must be kept ready for the Jews when someday they returned. I argued that at the moment the money might be of much greater use than at any other time. If they were caught and sent to concentration camps, the Jews would probably never get an opportunity to spend the capital according to the trust. Very likely, this kindly man answered regretfully, but nothing could be done about it. Moreover, the money was administered by a person of the highest rank, and, "You will no doubt understand that such a person cannot disregard his personal security and that of his head clerks, secretaries, clerks, and God-knows-what working at his office, and out of consideration for them he can't, of course, take upon himself any responsibility connected with illegal transactions of any kind!" When we asked him to tell us the name of the high-ranking man so we could apply to him, he regretted that he could not give the name, even as a favor, as he had promised not to reveal anything.

We left him with a deep feeling of dissatisfaction, and a feeling that the Christian "friends" of the Jews were, alas, not always fully aware of the seriousness of the situation. But it was—as a whole—rather difficult for us to understand why the capital needed could not be placed at our disposal from Jewish quarters. A well-known Copenhagen lawyer gave me the explanation of that once, when I fetched some money for the transports at his office: the fund concerned was not to be used to any great extent if it could be avoided, because it was not possible to find satisfactory excuses for sudden and large disbursements. And if the Germans learned that considerable Jewish capital, in trust for other purposes, had been spent in this way for refugees, it was most likely that they would confiscate all Jewish property immediately, as had happened in several other countries. I was very thankful for this information.

The answer with which our collectors of funds were sometimes dismissed—"Let the Jews themselves pay, let them help their own people, they have money enough"—might seem convincing. However, it was based on ignorance of the facts, as well as a less understandable and less pardonable lack of sympathy. The few times I heard that remark I saw before me a picture of people drowning, the old, the young, women and children, while at a suitable distance—so they were not annoyed by cries for help from the drowning people—a crowd of passive, though interested, onlookers said: Let them take care of themselves. What business is it of ours? They should have provided themselves with life preservers in time!

In any case, the present president of the Mosaic Religious Community in Denmark, Mr. Karl Lachmann, the managing director, has told me that he, together with the then president, Mr. C. B. Henriques, had sent an illegal message from Sweden to the non-Jewish administrator of the funds of the Mosaic Community, ordering him to pay two million kroner to support the Danish refugee organizations. The fact that the whole operation had to be carried out with economic support from other quarters cannot therefore be blamed on the Jews' own representatives.

As it is, the whole of this question must be viewed in connection with the special character of the persecutions of the Jews in Denmark. In contrast to those in the homeland of Nazism and several other countries occupied by the Germans where true autos-da-fé marked the culmination of a slow development of the continuous restriction of human and civil rights of the Jewish community, diabolic suddenness was employed in this country. Nobody could have foreseen with any degree of certainty what was going to take place in Hitler's "model protectorate," and the unfortunates were not given any chance whatsoever to take any joint precautions to prevent a situation which they knew—as in other countries—would occur almost as a historical necessity. Up to a few days before the raid, the highest Danish authorities advised the Jews not to attempt to arrange a general evacuation, in order not to risk rousing German suspicions and in that way provoking a persecution. The very thought of an organized flight had to be given up in advance as hopeless. The only country of refuge was Sweden, and all ships and smaller boats which were not being used for commercial purposes had been removed from the Danish coasts, as I have already indicated. And it was not until the persecutions had become an accomplished fact that the Swedish ambassador to Denmark, Gustaf von Dardel, persuaded his government to promise a sanctuary for all Danish Jews in Sweden. "We knew," writes Mr. Lachmann in a letter where he refers to this fact, "that Sweden had received a few score refugees—or maybe a hundred—but from that figure up to six thousand there is quite some distance. As long as we were all of us in Copenhagen it was impossible for us to know if Sweden would receive all the Danish Jews. I, for one, considered us lost."

There is still good reason to point out these facts

to those who think they know all the answers, and who now, as then, blame the Jews because they left others to do the rescue work. We tried to carry out the idea of letting the refugees themselves pay for one another during those first days of chaos and money shortage, in our own way. It was David—always full of ideas—who suggested the plan, and simple as it was I still consider it practical and under the circumstances absolutely justified. The Jews who wanted to pay for themselves as well as for their fellow sufferers gave us a power of attorney to dispose of their furniture and other property, and at the same time they handed over the keys to their homes and shops. One such power of attorney was sent to a Copenhagen lawyer, who had taken upon himself to arrange that sort of business for the Jews who feared that, as in Germany, their property might be confiscated by the Nazis when they left the country. In other cases we administered them ourselves. (It was primarily a question of furniture and second-hand goods belonging to David's family.) We collected the goods in a room at Faelled Road, and one of my co-workers, who runs a second-hand shop himself undertook the sorting and selling of the varied stock. Only things which we thought were of personal value were kept against the return of the Jews concerned. The money brought in by these sales was deposited temporarily in a secret account with the Bank of Lyngby, so that each individual owner had a certain number known only to the bank manager and me. But as it happened we very soon began to get money in other ways, and we left the amounts untouched, so that they would be at the disposal of the Jews when they returned—unless of course later on it should prove necessary to draw out these funds and spend them for the original purpose.

I do not deny that this aspect of our organization's activities was not wholly pleasant to me, although it was caused by the Jews themselves, and, under the circumstances, I considered it useful, let alone necessary. When I paid a visit to Mr. Henriques, the supreme court attorney I mentioned earlier, I asked him his opinion as a legal expert. I felt at once that he was rather doubtful, but I saw how his eyes grew bigger and bigger during my statement of the facts. All of a sudden he jumped up from his desk, patted me on the shoulder, and exclaimed cheerfully: "That's damned well the right thing to do." And then he gave me 7,000 kroner as a contribution to our work!

So in the end we got the money we needed from the refugees themselves, as well as through subscriptions and funds, private or official. We even got more than we needed. Among our contributors in this category I think of the physicians from Domus Medica and former Prime Minister Vilhelm Buhl with special gratitude. From the latter's apartment we received large sums. Often we were in a position to help and support other organizations and individual transports; for instance, we once paid 50,000 kroner to a ship at Islands Brygge in Copenhagen, and 55,000 kroner to an organization which took upon itself to take over our transports from Humlebæk. (I shall return to that later on.) One student received 10,000 kroner, the amount he lacked for a transport from Copenhagen. Dr. Gersfelt at Snekkersten, too, was provided with money on some occasions.

I shall have to say a little more about the episode of the student, as it offers an opportunity to give a needed explanation of one of the incidents in Dr. Gersfelt's book which illustrates the extreme relationship of trust existing among the helpers of the Jews. "One day," Dr. Gersfelt writes, "when it was announced at the Rockefeller Institute, where the entire staff headed by Professor Ege and his wife participated in the relief work, that a raid could be expected, all those who were involved left the laboratories and scattered all over the nearby park and along adjacent roads. The professor's wife, who was walking up and down Juliane Mary Road, was suddenly stopped by a man she did not know, who asked if she was Mrs. Ege. When she answered yes, he pulled 10,000 kroner out of his pocket, gave it to her, and disappeared. A few minutes afterwards another unknown man appeared, and the whole incident was repeated.

76

"Mrs. Ege went in behind a bicycle shed and hid the money in her stocking and resumed her very profitable walk. A little later a third man appeared. When he asked if she was Professor Ege's wife she looked forward to receiving more money. However, this man did not want to give her money—on the contrary. He was going to help some Jews to get out of the country himself and needed 10,000 kroner. He was told to turn round, and a moment later Mrs. Ege had conjured up the money he needed—much to his surprise."

I am in the fortunate position of being able to solve part of the mystery in this chapter of Denmark's modern history.

The story started at Norreport Subway Station. I had gone up to town at the request of a relative of one of the professors in the university, to try to get his wife across to Sweden. Just as I was leaving the station David, whom I had arranged to meet there, came up to me with a young student, who seemed to be in a state of great excitement. I gathered he was one of David's fellow students from the Agricultural High School, and now he had run into a bit of difficulty about getting money for a transport. He had twenty passengers. The ship was ready to leave from Langebro in Copenhagen, but the price was 20,000 kroner, and he had only 10,000. "Can't we get the money at once?" David said.

"Of course we can, but you will have to come along with me to the State Hospital," I answered, and hailed a taxi.

First I went to the university professor, whom I had originally come to see. "Where is your wife? We will get her across."

The professor told me that his wife had managed to get across the day before. He had just received a bunch of flowers from Sweden. That was the agreed sign telling him that she had had a successful crossing.

"Then let me have 10,000 kroner, please," I said. "Here is a student who needs it for his transport."

"I'd like to, if I had it. But I gave my wife all my available cash for her crossing," he answered. So we went up to see Professor Ege at the Institute of Physiology and I explained the matter to him. The professor turned his cigar box upside down; it only contained 3,500.

"Well, you must have a little patience," I told the student, "until we can get the money from Lyngby." I phoned my wife from the institute and asked her to send a man along with the amount. While we were waiting, Professor Ege showed me his files on the transport operations. They contained all the information you could possibly want in connection with relief work, everything expressed in chemical and physiological formulas after a system which would be sheer double Dutch to anybody but the inventor. Even if the Gestapo had had a host of physiologists and chemists to work on it, it would have been impossible for them to decipher these copious records.

Suddenly the alarm call was given all over the institute. A raid by the Hipos could be expected. (Hipo was the abbreviation for the German word *Hilfspolizei,* the Danish-German auxiliary police force.) We rushed down the back stairs and via strange routes reached the State Hospital. Besides the employees of the institute and the rest of us, there were also some Jews, who had been removed from their hiding place in the basement. I myself went to the casualty ward where I put on a doctor's white coat and snapped into action. I was given a hypodermic syringe and with the air of a professional doctor I approached a man with a bandaged arm, prepared to give him the injection against tetanus he was waiting for. Then all of a sudden it struck me that I had forgotten my hat and overcoat at the institute. In my coat there was a pocketbook which must not, under any circumstances, fall into the wrong hands. Probably this saved the patient's life—I had to give up both patient and syringe. Instead I got hold of a young doctor, who looked as if he had a better conscience than I had, and asked him to walk over to Professor Ege's office and get hold of my compromising belongings.

But there was still left unsolved the problem of the money for the student. The man with the bandaged arm completely vanished from my memory. With the institute occupied by the Hipos the messenger would walk right into the lion's den! I asked another of the doctors to go out and try to find a man who was bringing 10,000 kroner to Ege or me—that was all the description I could give him, because I did not know that my wife had sent Juel-Christensen, one of the chief props of our group, who specialized in finance. If I had known he was coming I would not have been at a loss for a description: tall, very stout, dark hair, rubicund, quiet, at first sight a bit phlegmatic. His slogan when joyfully and smilingly he patted his breast pocket and delivered money he had collected was: "Here's the dough! Kiss my cheek!"

Everything went all right. The first doctor returned dressed in my coat and with my hat doubled up in his inner pocket in place of my pocketbook and papers, which had been destroyed by a resolute doctor's assistant before she left the institute. Doctor No. 2 racked me a little longer. But he made up for that— when finally he showed up—by bringing me the student's greetings and thanks. He had met him in the hospital yard, quite beside himself with nervousness because of the money for the transport. Later on, when the doctor had been to the institute where he neither saw nor heard anything of the messenger from Lyngby, he ran into the student again, on his way to Langebro, jubilant, with the extra 10,000 kroner he had just got in his pocket.

Not until after my return from Sweden following the Liberation did I learn from the student, when one day I met him in the street, that the money had reached him in time and that the transport had been a success.

I heard nothing about Mrs. Ege's part in all this until I read Gersfelt's book. I regret that I have been able to solve only the mystery of the first 10,000 kroner. The details in connection with the second 10,000 must be left for future historiographers to clear up. It is out of the question that there could be any mistake in the narrative, as in my presence Mrs. Ege has confirmed that as a matter of fact the amount concerned was paid in twice. There is one possible explanation, and that is that a clerical error was made in Lyngby, and that as a result the amount was sent twice by two different persons. But I consider this theory most improbable. My wife, who was the life and soul of the enterprise at Buddinge Lane, as were Mrs. Ege and her husband at Juliane Mary Road, does not usually make mistakes. If quite exceptionally it happened that she made one, I hereby convey and transfer the 10,000 kroner to Professor Ege and his wife! As I have already mentioned we were in the closest possible connection all through October '43 and often exchanged both refugees and money. If I remember rightly, I finished up by owing Ege 25,000 kroner. Or vice versa—I forget. At any rate, the 10,000 can serve as an instalment. For the sake of order.

This short story which Gersfelt has caused me to revive and eke out has a sequel. As far as the student was concerned the visit to the State Hospital led to a continuation of his illegal work under Professor Ege and his wife, even after the transports had ceased. According to what he told me it resulted in a fractured skull on one occasion when he was being questioned by the Gestapo, and as the Germans did not like people to die in prison after cross examination treatments, he was sent to the hospital and subjected to a cerebral operation. He recovered and lived the rest of the war underground.

The way I left the scene of this drama was somewhat undignified but I include it for the sake of completeness and instruction. Having changed the token of my medical dignity, the white overall, for my own jacket and coat, I took a streetcar to go to 15 Faelled Road, where, as mentioned before, we had our shop for selling Jewish property. I had been to Humlebæk the night before and had had neither sleep nor food for twenty-four hours. That in connection with the excitement I had just gone through probably added up to the fact that all of a sudden I collapsed in the streetcar. I believe, though I regret it, that I fainted while standing on the rear platform. The kind conductor managed to restore me to consciousness—fortunately I was almost the only passenger—and as we had long ago passed Faelled Road he suggested that I should go on to Bispebjerg and there change to a No. 16 streetcar to Norrebro Street. I also remember that he helped me on board the streetcar at Bispebjerg. On my way from the tram halt to the shop of Larking, my co-worker, I felt ill again, and I probably looked more than exhausted when finally I arrived at the shop. At any rate Larking and his wife treated me with the greatest care, placed me in the room behind the shop on a soft couch of second-hand goods, old clothes from the Jewish properties under our administration, and poured a tumbler of straight Scotch whiskey down my throat. It is a drink I have always detested. But then I realized that its effects can be almost magical: I felt my strength grow and my courage return, and life appeared before me in the most bright and happy colors. It is still impossible for me to understand the attraction of whiskey as a thing you can drink for pleasure. It reminds me too unpleasantly of a very hot and obstinate stove I had to stoke in my early youth. But as a medicine! For that purpose I can certainly recommend it from the bottom of my heart —as the last, encouraging result of my personal experiences of that memorable day.

IV

The Racketeers

IT COULD HARDLY have been avoided, considering the conditions under which the relief work was carried on, that certain temptations were offered to those with a wavering strength of character. Still, the danger of loss through treachery was not as great as one might imagine. The group of colleagues consisted almost exclusively of people I knew well myself or of people about whom I had received information guaranteeing their reliability. The funds for the transports were administered from the main office at Buddinge Lane, headed by my wife, and the money was collected at Humlebæk by the management at the Hotel Gylfe, and every time money was paid out a personal, oral receipt was given. Nevertheless, during the first exciting days of the persecution there were a few examples of people who wanted to fish to their own profit in troubled waters. Yet within the work of the Lyngby Group itself there were only a couple of instances of fraudulent behavior.

84

A young man with a strange foreign name, Mr. L., came out to Buddinge Lane one day and asked if he could borrow money for a boat, which was to be used by the Students' Group at Regensen (a student dormitory since 1623). He was a member of the group there from which we had had a good deal of co-operation. My wife had the money, but as she did not know the man she refused to lend him anything for the time being, and referred the matter to me for examination when I got home. I phoned Regensen several times, but nobody from the group was at home. As I knew the man from the work at Humlebæk, and as my impression of him from up there suggested no possible reason why I should suspect him, I told my wife to pay the money to him if he came back while I was away, but to ask him to give a detailed description of what the money was needed for. Here, as in other cases, we were faced with two alternatives: should we risk the money——or the lives of the Jews? In this case we backed the wrong horse. The "student" got the money, amounting to 20,000 kroner, and was told to repay it as soon as his group could afford it, and further, to give us a report of the results of the transport as soon as possible. A couple of days afterwards, when we had not heard a word from him, I went up to Regensen. This time I managed to meet the leaders of the group, Langhoff and Kildebye, two students. None of them knew anything at all about the young man with the strange name, and the group had not asked for any money from Lyngby.

If the fellow had not been as foolish as he was bold it is very likely that he might have kept all this money. At that time the conditions of a search for persons who had defrauded an illegal organization were of course not exactly favorable. Provisionally I told my wife to ask Mr. L. to come out to Lyngby if he should phone for more money, and then I went down to the police and reported what had happened. I did not do so until after careful consideration and a good deal of hesitation. Because of the nature of the case publicity was undesirable, obviously. Neither my wife nor I could afford the time for long interviews with the police. The police reassured me on both points. They promised me that the entire case would be treated in strictest confidence, that the report would contain nothing at all about the Lyngby Group or the transports, and that the police would see to it that, if they considered him dangerous, the pseudo student would be rendered harmless either by keeping him imprisoned as long as necessary, or, if need be, by sending him to Sweden to let the Swedish police intern him till after the war.

For the present, the point was to get hold of the fellow. The great difficulty was that I could not remember his strange name quite correctly, so the scrutiny of records and files which started immediately was bound to be fruitless. For the moment we could only hope that he would call at Buddinge Lane. Then it would be an easy matter for the police to take care of him.

Just at the moment when I was down at the police station there came a phone call from L. to Buddinge Lane. He mentioned something about another transport. My wife suggested that he should come to fetch the money the same afternoon, but she did not tell him that on that occasion he would be introduced to two new members of the group, a couple of detectives from the criminal police. Nor did it happen that way, either. Only a few hours after my application to the police two detectives came down to Buddinge Lane and showed us a picture, taken from three different angles, which they had found in their files.

"That's right, that's the one," I said.

The same afternoon he was arrested in Nansens Street, where he had agreed to meet one of my colleagues. When he was questioned and his rooms were searched it was discovered that 10,000 of the 20,000 kroner was left. He said 8,000 had actually been spent on a transport, and his statement on this point was so detailed that the police found no reason to doubt its correctness. The remaining 2,000 kroner had been spent on different "extras" connected with the transport, he maintained. He was very repentant, wept, and accused himself of being the most wretched man on earth, worthy of the contempt of all decent people.

L.'s former differences with the police had been in the line of embezzlement and insurance fraud. In this new case the police thought that the fright he had had in Nansens Street when he was arrested was so serious that he would not be a danger to us in the future. They therefore suggested that we should consider the case settled. We, on our part, had every reason to do just as little about it as the police thought fit, and were very pleased that most of the money had been recovered, or at least spent to good purpose by this false servant of our cause.

Supported by previous reports on him, the police had the impression that L. was not actually a criminal by nature, but a weak character, a dreamer with psychopathic tendencies. In Humlebæk he had often proved useful. As a whole I am convinced now that when he was working on the coast he was really inspired by a will to help the persecuted. With people like him it was usually not until "the day after the night before," under the conditions of everyday, normal life, that the thought of the enormous amounts of money circulating came into the foreground, superseding their sympathy for the poor, unhappy victims. Then the idea of "pulling a fast one" on the organization would materialize.

Far more dangerous and much more unattractive than this neurotic were the sharks in human form who followed in the wake of the Jews and cynically exploited their misfortune. They form an element in the picture which should not be veiled, but it would be extremely unfortunate if it overshadowed the true spirit of the transports: that is, that here Danish men and women from all walks of life were united for unselfish work in the service of mankind.

Toward the end of October we somehow learned that seven Jews from the county of Humlebæk had been defrauded of 21,000 kroner in connection with a transport. Although the matter did not concern the Lyngby Group directly—as far as we knew the transport had been effected before we started from up there—we still considered ourselves obliged to investigate the matter. We succeeded in getting the names and addresses of the two skippers who had made the trip, and we sent them a message telling them to appear at the Bellevue Seaside Hotel. They were summoned to appear at 11:30 sharp, and in laconic terms they were induced to believe that the best thing they could do was to comply with the order—or else. Believe it or not, they showed up— right on time! A court-martial was set up immediately, in a room very well suited for the purpose and placed at our disposal by the manager of the hotel.

Besides the two "accused" there were five members of the group present. The defendants seemed to be rather unpleasantly affected by the situation. They were very nervous, and we thought that their eyes gave away their bad consciences. But this was not a place where judgment should be based on feelings and vague impressions. Strict justice—personified by one manufacturer, two merchants, one hotel porter, and one lecturer—set to work instantaneously. One merchant acted as magistrate and president of the court, and the rest were the jury. All were wrapped in a cloud of silence, now and then slashed by questions, cutting like lightning through ominous darkness.

Unexpectedly the accused pleaded guilty—and that without any use of revolvers, thumbscrews, or other of the implements introduced by the cross-examination technique of the Gestapo, though the looks of the accused seemed to indicate that they expected them. As a result we got a pleasant and surprising explanation. It appeared, as a matter of fact, that our spontaneous judgment of our two countrymen had been completely wrong. In reality they were just as gentle and as innocent in intrigue as doves. Their only offense was that in this particular case they had been almost as simple-minded as the birds of peace. And after all this could not really be considered an offense. It could rather be said, perhaps, that they had been the victims of unfortunate circumstances, for which they could not possibly be held responsible—according to them. An arrangement had been made, they went on, for the seven Jews to be sailed over to Sweden on a night trip at a total fare of 25,000 kroner. Quite a nice price, but also a nice boat—and with nice skippers! Time and place for the departure had been fixed, and the money paid. Then ill luck would have it that their engines broke down so they were prevented from sailing that night. And what was worse, their agent on land played a trick on the un-suspecting skippers and made a new agreement with the same Jews for a new crossing the following day, and this time the fares were cheaper, 21,000 kroner. In short, when—with peace in their minds, the kind of peace in which a good conscience is such an in-evitable ingredient—they returned from Sweden after a well-executed operation they discovered much to their amazement that they had 21,000 kroner more in their wallets than they ought to have under the original agreement.

How extremely annoying! We understood that this unfortunate mishap had almost entirely spoiled the satisfaction they felt at the good deed they had done. For what should they do with the money? The Jews were in Sweden, weren't they, so it was absolutely impossible to pay it back.

At this point we thought we ought to step in to offer our assistance. We suggested that they should let us have the money. Then we would see to it that it was repaid to their passengers, if not before, then on their return to Denmark. But alas—what else could be expected after so much bad luck: the money was not at the disposal of the two skippers any more.

91

In their despair they had invested it in a boat and a house. Now we had really run into trouble. What could we do about it?

We advised them to sign a document, which—strangely enough—had been set up and typed beforehand. It contained a declaration to the effect that jointly they had received 21,000 kroner more than they had agreed upon for the crossing, and that they wanted—or rather bound themselves—to pay 10,500 kroner each in twelve monthly instalments to Mr. Federspiel, High Court Attorney.

Strangely enough, they did not seem to be very pleased, or even relieved, when they signed. That did disappoint us a little, but it did not prevent us from taking the solemn declaration to Mr. Federspiel. The reason we picked him was that a few days previously I had had a conversation with him in his office, and it was then revealed that he, too, had worked on the transport operations. Mr. Federspiel in person received the document and promised to collect the money from our two friends.

I did not see these men for two years, and I wish that I had never seen them again. Then I could finish the story here with the moral, which I also took down in my notes about them in Sweden shortly after our meeting. At that time I had enjoyed the episode at the Bellevue as "an example of how a closer examination of a crude story about a swindle may lead to an explanation which shows that people may be better than expected." Now, however, I must finish it in the interests of truth, and then put it away in my rather comprehensive archive of false illusions.

When we met the second time, the circumstances were exactly the same as when we had met at the Bellevue, apart from the difference in conditions caused by the fact that now we were back again under normal legal procedures. Once again the scene was a law court, but this time it was the City of Copenhagen Court. The actors were real judges and jurors, there was a Counsel for the Prosecution as well as a Counsel for the Defense, and I had been summoned as a witness.

At first glance the accused men seemed unchanged to me. As before they were sinister-looking, and appeared to be troubled by bad consciences and presentiments of evil, but this time their features did not light up during the proceedings, probably because there were no grounds for a more cheerful view of things. The case was the same as in 1943, but new incidents had been added to the proceedings at the Bellevue, and it was the continuation of the story which was the serious part.

Almost simultaneously with the meeting at the Bellevue the Swedish Broadcasting Corporation had sent out a message about the seven Jews who had been defrauded by two Danish skippers during a crossing to Sweden. At that time people on the other side of the Sound had not learned that the illegal transports had to be treated with reticence. Among other details the names and addresses of the two skippers had been given in the news bulletin. The result was, of course, that the skippers were arrested by the German police, not because they had any intention of helping the defrauded Jews to get their money back, but because the Germans thought that now they might get information about an underground route.

During their stay in prison the two Danes learned that Mr. Federspiel was among the prisoners of the same jail. For the second time he had been arrested under suspicion of illegal activity, and here the two distinguished mariners saw their big chance. They reported Federspiel as a member of our group, and in that way managed to get rid of the unpleasant claim for 21,000 kroner, and at the same time obtained a very useful stock of good will with the German police. A search of the attorney's office brought the I.O.U. to light, unfortunately at a most unfavorable time for Mr. Federspiel. Up to then the evidence against him had been very weak, but now here was a proof in black and white of his anti-German activity. The result was as could be expected: the informers were set free and Federspiel sent to Froslev, the German concentration camp in Southern Jutland. But here again, as so often in those days, the sequel made things even. The two crooks, who had both of them been punished before, were sentenced to four and five years respectively by the City Court, and if I remember correctly an appeal for a more severe sentence was lodged with the High Court by the government.

On my return from Sweden, when I read about the case in the papers, I phoned Mr. Federspiel and regretted that in my capacity as the leader of the Lyngby Group I had contributed—in a sense—toward the trouble he had run into with the Germans. Mr. Federspiel answered that he personally had promised his assistance, and therefore his was the responsibility and the risk. I was indeed pleased to hear him say that.

What happened to the seven Jews and their money seems to me to be less important today. I hope that they have received it, and if not, then I hope that they have managed to live without it. On the other hand, one might also say that 21,000 kroner was a moderate fine for such foolishness as passing on information of that kind to the Swedish Broadcasting Corporation.

The whole question of money came up all too often. Several years after the war when I visited a friend and close colleague from the Lyngby Group I heard about an embarrassing talk he had had with a Jewish lady who had been one of the passengers of the "Big Transport" of 230 persons from Humlebæk.

"She maintained," he said, "that you had walked around and induced the Jews to pay more than the

500 kroner which was the fare, pretending that in Sweden the Danish krone was not worth more than seven hundredths of one krone. Of course, I told her that this couldn't possibly be right. She must remember it wrong. And it is not true, is it?"

"No," I said, "it is not quite true. We did not say the rate of exchange was seven hundredths. We said it was four hundredths. It is extremely probable that in that way we collected several thousand extra kroner at Humlebæk."

My friend looked at me doubtfully. I think he was a bit shaken. "That sounds fantastic," he said, "but at any rate, it was said in good faith, wasn't it?"

"As far as I remember, yes. It was something we thought we knew, a rumor which was in the air up there, and we considered it quite true. But apart from that—even if we had known that it was not right, I expect that we should have said so all the same under those circumstances. But let us try and ask David, to hear what he says," I suggested, "or Norrild."

He readily agreed to choose those two as our moral court of appeal. I phoned David.

"Do you remember that the first nights at Humlebæk when we were collecting the money we said that the Danish krone was of almost no value in Sweden?"

"I do."

"How much did we say was the rate of exchange over there?"

"Four hundredths."

"Did you know, at that time, if it was correct?"

"As far as I remember, it was in good faith, but I suppose that we would have said so anyway, if it had been necessary. What else could we do? We couldn't let other people get caught and taken to Germany just because they could not afford to pay for their flight!"

Norrild's answer was absolutely in conformity with David's. It even appeared to me that there was a tinge of indignation in it that anybody could have the slightest doubt as to the justification of our line of action under those circumstances.

"Everything changes," said the learned Heraclitus. That goes for civil laws and time-honored moral standards, too. He who works toward the welfare of mankind must fight evil, which employs all means, and, consequently, he himself must--under certain circumstances—take the responsibility of employing means whose justification may be doubted later by those who did not experience the situation concerned. A heavy responsibility and a dangerous doctrine, not unlike the so-called jesuitical one: "The end justifies the means."

In those days even the custodians of the law opposed the law. The police offered to imprison people without preliminary examination, and took criminals out of prison contrary to law and order, clergymen and doctors issued false certificates, apothecaries

97

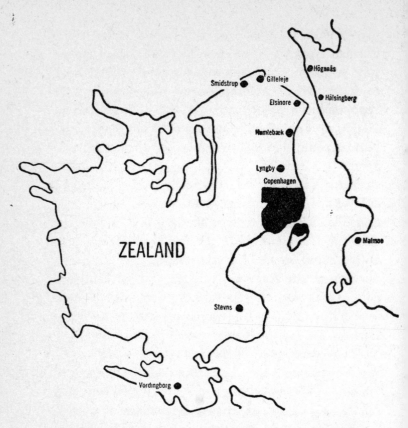

filled prescriptions for drugs without regard to statutory regulations. These facts will probably be understood and forgiven, even by the strictest moralists. But many will find it hard to understand that, also for the sake of the Jews, people taught their children to lie; and that under certain circumstances people even considered it imperative to cheat those whom they wanted to help. And law-abiding people, who learned about the crazy way we were forced by the state of affairs to handle money, naturally felt open to doubts. When a man to whom 100 kroner usually represents a considerable amount starts spending 10,000 as if it were small change, it will always appear somewhat queer, even to himself; and very few people will later be able to remember or fully understand the confused and fantastic situation which necessitated such a line of action. There were others than the helpers of the Jews who were busy those days: the self-appointed guardians of morals, the always eager—and always passive—critics, who were outside and knew everything better, the scandalmongers and gossips of the type who said: "It's absolutely true! Somebody said so at the grocer's at Hellerup!"

Those who helped the Jews and whose illegal work often resulted in loss of their property and freedom, or several years of exile, deprived of their family, friends, and jobs, have lived to hear their personal honesty called into question by complete strangers. When all is said and done, the danger that a man's good reputation in civil life should be impaired forever was probably the greatest risk to which those who fought the Gestapo in the service of Jewish relief, were exposed. If it is at all possible to say that in the days of the persecution of the Jews their Danish fellow citizens made sacrifices, then this was no doubt one of the heaviest.

99

V

The Humlebaek Route

Humlebæk deserves a page in the history of the relief work during the persecution of the Jews, just as previously it played an important part in the history of Denmark. It was at Humlebæk that the Swedish King, Charles XII, and his army landed during the Great Scandinavian War in 1700. In 1943 the beach up there became the starting-point of a Danish invasion of Sweden. A different kind of invasion, but one which probably was no less exciting or less hazardous.

In several respects the place seemed to be ideal for illegal transports. There the Sound is comparatively narrow, and normally it takes a fishing vessel only about three-quarters of an hour to cross into Swedish territorial waters north of the island of Hveen. It is true that the harbor of Humlebæk itself was not suitable for illegal and secret embarkations as it was subject to German control, but jetties and small bridges along the coast proved highly useful for our purpose. In particular the long pier at the brick works at Nivaa experienced a renaissance of traffic far beyond expectation.

Consequently, it was not strange that many Jews went up there on their own, especially after it had become necessary to give up the routes farther south. Normally a good route across the Sound could be used only for a couple of days. As soon as traffic increased, the Germans' suspicion followed suit, and it was necessary to move the whole operation. As far as I know, there had been some transports from the Humlebæk area before we moved up there from Lyngby, but they had been few and far between, and only small parties had been sent across. It was obvious that a well-planned organization would be imperative if we were to succeed in sending across the hundreds of refugees who were waiting along the coast, in Humlebæk itself, and in the hayloft already mentioned.

The first night we were up there, there was no crossing as far as I know, at any rate it did not amount to much. The Jews had to stay overnight and the following few days in their hide-out, and the endeavors of their helpers had to be concentrated first on providing for the refugees and, second, on preparing their embarkation in the course of the following nights, with due regard both to safety and the greatest possible number we could send. Mr. Norrild and his wife managed to get hold of some members of the Women's Voluntary Service, who provided food for the Jews in the loft, and in other places where they had not been billeted on the villagers. Special difficulties in connection with the distinctive features of the orthodox Jewish bill of fare were solved as well as circumstances permitted. The rationing then generally in force caused no trouble as all the refugees handed over their coupons, realizing that whatever came of our attempt to save them they would not need the coupons for a long while.

The following night we had not yet succeeded in organizing any large-scale transport. Only a couple of small fishing vessels took passengers from among the Jews who could afford to pay their way. I remember that while I was at Lyngby I received a phone call from somebody in the house in Station Avenue at Humlebæk, who requested that I should come up there at once and bring along 3 kroner for movie tickets. Deciphered, this telephone parlance of ours meant that I should bring 3,000 kroner to pay for a crossing. I left immediately. When I got up there with the 3,500 kroner we had collected that day at Lyngby, I found the small family who had asked for the money lost in despair. A fisherman had been there and offered them seats in his boat if they would pay 1,000 kroner each. As they did not have the money, they had phoned Lyngby instead of applying to some of the members of the group who were in the same village, even in the same house. So now I was too late, and they could not go to the movies that night—others had bought the tickets. I did my best to console them and promised that they would get across as soon as we could find room for them. As was normally the case, they soon calmed down and were silent again.

It was quite striking to notice the difference between the Jews in the crowded rooms in Station Avenue and the group I had left early in the morning in the hayloft. In contrast with the strange, peaceful silence in which the others jointly and unanimously put up with their fate, the entire atmosphere in this house was characterized by the utmost despair and nervousness. The room resounded with weeping and crying, mixed with a monotonous murmur of prayers in Hebrew. However, here, too, my previous experiences were proved right: a simple promise, put forward in a firm and convincing tone, that we would help them, had an almost magic effect. The Jews became quiet and apparently confident. Nobody asked where we got such confidence, and nobody seemed to suspect that our hopes were just as vague and unfounded as their own despair was real and horrible.

In one of the rooms I ran into a passionate domestic scene. Two families had made arrangements with a fisherman for a crossing. His boat could just hold the eight of them, and the price was 10,000 kroner. As they had only 8,500 among them, they

103

asked me to give them the necessary 1,500. One of
the families consisted of a young married couple and
their baby daughter, and I noticed at once that the
wife was not a Jew. I also understood from their conversation that she did not really want to leave. To
her husband's great despair I therefore refused to pay
the money, explaining that the funds at my disposal
were meant only to help Jews. At the moment only
those of completely Jewish blood were in direct danger, and consequently I was in no position to help
the young woman and her child. But I would be willing to pay the extra money if they would let two Jews
go instead. I also promised the husband, who told
me that he had given notice to his landlord that he
would quit his apartment and that they had sold their
furniture to raise money for the crossing, that I would
take care of his wife and child and guarantee their
subsistence till they could all meet again.

My offer only increased his exasperation. "Will
you take the responsibility of separating a father
from his child and wife?" he shouted accusingly.
And with sobs, when I answered that under present
circumstances I would have to take full responsibility, he refused to leave.

"Then I prefer the gas-chamber!" he cried, beating his head and arms against the wall in a state of
great emotion.

The wife, on the contrary, was strikingly calm. I

104

even thought that I sensed a certain amount of contempt in her voice when she told him,

"Of course you must go. You will get along all right in Sweden without us, just wait and see."

She was quite right, and he soon came to his senses. With two of the other Jews present serving as substitutes, the party now received the 1,500 kroner they needed. Some time afterwards I learned that they did not get across that night after all, but joined one of our transports a couple of nights later.

The following night the Lyngby Group embarked its first transport from the shores of the Sound. Shortly after I arrived back at the hayloft from the house in Station Avenue we received a message from a contact in Elsinore that it would be possible for quite a number of Jews to get across the same night from a certain place on the sea front. It was estimated that eleven boats, each with room for fifteen, could be sent across. The refugees could be taken to the place of embarkation by trucks, two of which had been placed at our disposal from Humlebæk.

Among many other pictures I remember from those days, the scene at the farm near Humlebæk that night is still so vivid that it will never be obliterated. We had to load the big truck with people as if they were cattle or sacks of produce. We lifted them up and hauled them, all of them, aged, women, and babies, across the high backboard or sideboards, and placed them crouching or flat on the bottom of the truck, one on top of the other, so that no one was visible above the sides of the truck. Everything took place in deepest silence, without a complaint, but the very fact that with apparent cold-bloodedness we treated human beings as if they were animals or inert matter gave this sinister scene a touch of horror. The surroundings, too, played their part: the gloomy barn, the darkness of the October night, faintly dispelled by a rising moon behind rain clouds and the gleam from the lantern in the half-open stable door.

We wanted nothing more than to help these people. Yet the words from Isaiah (LIII, 7) kept entering my mind: *He was oppressed, and he was afflicted, yet he opened not his mouth: he is brought as a lamb to the slaughter, and as a sheep before her shearers is dumb, so he openeth not his mouth.*

I think that that night I experienced what it means to hate—even more strongly than on any other occasion. I hated our oppressors because they made us treat human beings in that way and forced us into the degradation of having to smuggle Danish fellow citizens out of our own country as if they were criminals. At the same time I was worried all during the endless drive along the sea front through Elsinore by the constant thought: What will happen if the Gestapo shows up? Unarmed as we were we had no possibility of preventing the Germans—even if there were only two of them—from arresting all the Jews.

Today—eight years afterwards—I can still feel the entire complex of sorrow, hatred, fear, and the crushing feeling of guilt and powerlessness under a predominant responsibility, which filled me that night on our way to Sommariva.

When we arrived at the place appointed in the message we had received, we found only two young men who invited us into the entrance hall. The trucks with the Jews were left outside in the street. However, we were very much disappointed as soon as we got into the house: not eleven but only *one* boat was ready, and it could hold only about ten passengers. The price was 15,000 kroner, and it must be paid before the embarkation. We were rather short of money and my colleague, Bjarne Sigtryggsson, who —being a practical businessman—led the negotiations and declared at once that the terms were unacceptable. After a brief dispute he settled the whole case by placing 10,000 kroner on the table and hammering his fist down on the heap with a bang, "This is as much as you will get—and not a penny more. So it is up to you whether to sail or not!"

Apparently Sig's tactics were right. Of course the fishermen were just as interested in getting their boat filled up now that it was there as we were, and without further discussion their representatives ashore agreed to our offer. The money was paid, and we went outside to pick out the passengers. I explained the situation to the Jews, and suggested that

107

the family with the many children should be the first. Nobody had any objections to this, and when we found out that there was room for a few more the family of three, to whom I had promised the night before that they would be saved as soon as possible, was selected. That made fifteen or sixteen Jews in all, and they were now led through the garden of Mr. Parkov, the brewery manager, and down to the narrow boat landing from which they were taken in rowboats to the waiting fishing vessel.

This was the first time we had seen our Jewish friends actually entering a boat and sailing off toward the Swedish coast, which with its gleaming and brilliant lights drew the Jews just as centuries ago the Promised Land had attracted their forefathers. Nobody who has not attended an embarkation of that kind will be able to imagine the feelings that overcome those who are left behind and see the heavily loaded ship sailing off toward safety and freedom. Mingled are rage at human wickedness, sympathy and grief at the misfortunes of the persecuted, the excitement, the uncertainty, and the painful responsibility—above all the responsibility—but also the duty, and an elevating and strengthening feeling of friendship and solidarity of the task. Everything is dissolved into a strange, indescribable feeling of happiness when the work is finished.

While we were walking up the landing afterwards and the two young men were wading ashore, I noticed that one of them was weeping. From the beginning I had felt very little sympathy for him and his friend, and I did not quite believe in his assurances that it was only the skipper who was interested in the high price. Now I stretched my hand out to him and thanked him for helping us. He rested the other hand on my shoulder and exclaimed, "It's damnable, unbearable. Poor souls—those beasts of Germans! Take care of yourself or they will get you. Here's my address. If you get in trouble, come up here. We will get you across, and it won't cost you a penny!" That was the way he felt, this unknown friend from Elsinore. I have forgotten his name, and I threw his address away. But I shall always remember him.

The trucks with the remaining Jews had started for Humlebæk at once to see if there were any possibility of getting across there, or, if they were not successful, to return them to the shelter of the hayloft. I myself went to Elsinore with a colleague to try to raise more money for our work. We had about 20,000 kroner in all, but we realized that it would be quite insufficient if in the course of the night there should be such numerous and large transports to send off as might be hoped for after our first bit of luck. My intentions were that despite the late hour we should make an attempt to get in touch with the commercial banks or savings banks in Elsinore, and try to induce them to provide us with another twenty or thirty thousand kroner by explaining the situation to the managers. We would offer the same security as to Mr. Fog in Lyngby a couple of days previously— only a confident hope that the money would probably be repaid one way or another. It is true that I did not know any of the "capitalists" in question— for that matter, I did not know anybody at all in Elsinore.

For the time being I could only hope that someone in the school system there would help us and understand our troubles. So we tried to get hold of the headmaster of the Elsinore High School, Mr. V. A. C. Jensen. It turned out to be rather a difficult job for the driver to locate his home in the darkness. Eventually we did find the headmaster's villa, and he did not let us down. Mr. Jensen and his wife received us cordially, and when I explained the reason for our visit the headmaster did not consider it by any means absurd. He promised to help us. While his wife was serving tea he phoned the different managers of the local financial institutions one after the other to ask them to come and take care of some new customers. Unfortunately none of them was at home. It was the first night after the curfew had been lifted, and evidently the occasion was being celebrated in influential circles of the town. The headmaster did not know the social connections of these money-men, and therefore sent for the local inspector who he thought might be better informed. But that gentleman was equally unsuccessful when he tried to find them by telephone. It seemed a great pity.

It is quite likely that their rejoicing at the recovered freedom for social intercourse would not have been increased if the headmaster had asked them if they would mind stopping by the bank to pick up 25,000 kroner and bring them along to a man from Lyngby who was temporarily short of cash. Would we have got it at all? I pass what is so far an unanswered question on to those concerned. At the bottom of my heart I think we would—at least I thought so at that time. In those days everything was possible when it was a question of helping the persecuted Jews—even that otherwise inconceivable thing: that a bank should grant a loan without security.

I got back to Humlebæk around midnight, and after some looking around I found the rest of the members of the group on the beach. Our attempt to establish a connection across the Sound in the course of the night proved fruitless, apart from the one small transport. Our spirits were running low when sometime about dawn Sig and I went into the Hotel Gylfe to get a little sleep. A couple of hours later when I was about to get on the early morning train for Lyngby I woke Sig and asked him to come along into the next room where two other members of the group were sleeping. We also sent for Villumsen, the landlady's son, and we then held a brief bedside council of war.

111

I suggested that we should now organize the work at Humlebæk all over from scratch, and I advised that we should elect a leader with full local authority, to be responsible only to the organization in Lyngby. I was very pleased when the other three at once and unanimously appointed Sig. I could not think of a better solution considering my impression of this young man through the last few eventful nights and days.

From then on the operation was more thoroughly planned and the speed increased. The interest of the local people was activated. Many young boys served as guards, messengers, guides, and in the information service. The Jews who were not billeted on the villagers were quartered at the brick works at Nivaa. Our own Jews, too, were moved from their safe but far too remote hayloft, to the brick works of Mr. Olsen.

These huge buildings were very well suited for the purpose. They were hardly more comfortable than the loft, but with their many dark rooms they offered good hiding places, and above all they were quite near the place of embarkation. How the bricks in the works could be used to hide the inmates under critical conditions is described later on in this book by Mr. Jens Nyskov.

Now the connection between the fishermen and the skippers and the group became more established, time and places for embarkations were fixed, and so were the prices. The flow of Jews, too, was regulated. For a couple of days, for instance, no more Jews were sent up from Lyngby. They remained in their quarters there instead until Humlebæk was relieved of its surplus population.

The biggest crossings were made in a schooner belonging to a dealer in traprock. He told me that he had once been a diver in North Africa and had dug up an adventure or two. During the Spanish Civil War he had sailed for two years with the same ship, alternately chartered by Franco and "the Reds." He had not been hampered by any irrelevant political considerations, and his business had flourished. At one time he had been worth two million kroner—he said. Three months later he had not a cent left. It is to be supposed that the Transports had revived him economically; at any rate he soon realized that it was more profitable to ship Jews than stone—and here again he had no difficulty in assuming merely a businesslike viewpoint free of sentimental considerations. On the other hand, he was not unreasonable as regards prices—500 kroner per person—and he even granted a discount on cargoes of considerable size. For the transport on the night of October 8th-9th —the one which the group usually referred to as the "Big Transport"—he received 100,000 kroner only, although it was well known that there were 230 passengers on board. But then again it was a question whether he would ever sail at all! When his ship was

113

to leave the Nivaa pier at midnight the engine would not start, and up until five o'clock in the morning the ship was still rolling off the pier with its cargo of human beings in its holds. No wonder that by then the nerves of both the Jews and their helpers on shore were stretched to the breaking-point. It was not till late in the night that we managed to get hold of a local man, an old fishing skipper, who both could and would help.

The "Big Transport," which is probably the biggest and most dramatic operation in the history of the Danish Jew Transports, is described more fully in Mr. Jens Nyskov's contribution later in this book. He participated in it as the representative of the Lyngby Group.

The fishing skipper who helped us to start the engine had been promised 25,000 kroner extra, to be paid by the master of the schooner, but when the crossing had been successfully completed the latter refused to pay. Eventually, we had to settle the matter by paying the fisherman what money we ourselves had left, 17,000 kroner. So one single crossing cost us 117,000 kroner in all.

The Nivaa skipper's claim on the illegal skipper of stones in Humlebæk is not the only dubious thing in connection with this memorable character. In one of his novels Holberg, our great poet of the eighteenth century, writes that in France he once had the pleasure of traveling for two days with a Mexican ex-pirate, "and I learned a lot from him that is either not to be found in books or is not dealt with there sufficiently and thoroughly." Holberg would have enjoyed my Mexican in Humlebæk to an even higher degree. There is no doubt that he was a useful man to us. He had a ship, and he was willing to sail. And in between he was able to spin a yarn in his singing island dialect about the vicissitudes of his life, quite as fascinating as that of any pirate. I think that what has been published—especially in newspaper accounts from the Supreme Court of his exploits during the fight for freedom in the latter part of the Occupation—has been dealt with "sufficiently and thoroughly." So here I am only going to describe his activities in the service of the relief work for the Jews, as a brief contribution to the history of this strange period.

As for the "Big Transport" I must refer to Mr. Nyskov's account. I myself have nothing to tell. That night I was in my bed in Lyngby, having swallowed a maximum dose of sleeping pills in order to neutralize the effects of stimuli which had kept me up and about for days on end without much sleep.

As far as I remember, my Mexican made four crossings in all for our group in Humlebæk. The last time was the one I just mentioned. For one of the other crossings he received 70,000 kroner. The morning after the dramatic night when Norrild and Prior, who had both been present on the beach, told me about it, I went right over to see the manager of Burmeister & Wain, the shipbuilding firm, who lived almost right across the street at Buddinge Lane, and told him about the obstinate engine. The very same morning Mr. Carstensen, the manager, sent one of the staff up to Humlebæk, and later the whole ship was surveyed by none other than Professor Prohaska, who teaches shipbuilding at the Technical High School. He approved of its condition. It was an old windjammer which had been scrapped by its former owners. The skipper himself stated that he had bought it for 25,000 kroner. It would seem that he had no reason to complain, either of the payment or of the technical service he and his ship were offered by the group. But he did, at any rate of the first item. About seven years after we worked together at Humlebæk I received a letter in which he asked me to put forward a proposal for settlement of my debt to him in connection with his activity in Humlebæk.

It was not only the engine breakdown which made us think carefully about making a change in the method of transport. Lately the Gestapo divisions from Elsinore had made the coast around our embarkation places unsafe, and although—contrary to our habit—we had safeguarded the "Big Transport" by means of armed Danish policemen and could reckon on similar support in the future, we had a feeling that the situation was coming to a head. Did we dare to go on taking the responsibility of joint transports on such a large scale, or should we go back to using smaller boats, with correspondingly smaller risk? Or should we move to another and less dangerous place on the Sound or the Kattegat? Or would it be better to leave the transports to other organizations—that is, if we could find them, and if they were able and willing to undertake the work and assume responsibility—and in that way ease the burden which was oppressing us more and more every day?

The following Sunday (October 10) I had a prolonged discussion with the Mexican. I think he had a hunch that I contemplated moving the business, and now he offered his services right to the end. At Olsen's brick works there were at this time sixty-seven Jews, who had arrived after the "Big Transport," and he suggested that we should take them across the very same afternoon. He admitted that there was quite a strong wind blowing, almost a gale, so it would be impossible to row across to the ship from the pier, but he recommended a method under which it would be possible to haul the rowboats across by means of ropes—and as far as I understood it would be easy and without risk. I took up an attitude of absolute refusal. For one thing, we did not embark in the daytime, I said. For another, we would take no chances again, especially in an easterly gale, and finally, I was contemplating a rearrangement of the entire transport work after the incidents the previous night.

It was obvious that the Mexican was disgusted and disappointed at my hesitation. Whether it was primarily due to his feelings toward the Jews, or whether he was thinking of the 35,000 kroner he would not be able to lay his hands on, I cannot say for certain, but I am not disinclined to believe in the latter possibility. Neither my colleagues nor I had ever noticed that he had any special interest in his passengers—but plenty in their money. Here, as in Spain during the Civil War, he was evidently working in accordance with the good old principle: business is business. There was quite a little coolness in the air between us when we parted.

Immediately after this conversation a customs house assistant called on me at the Gylfe. He was from Humlebæk and had been with us previously as a useful helper during the transports, and now he informed us that he had a good and safe new connection to Sweden. A mechanic up there had been given the job of repairing one of the German PT boats. He had almost finished the work by now, and the following Tuesday the boat was going on a trial trip without passengers, but the mechanic thought that it might as well be of some use in the meantime. If we would keep the Jews ready at the pier Tuesday afternoon he would come alongside and take them to Helsingborg.

Not a bad idea at all, I thought. To send Danish Jews to Sweden in a German PT boat—if that did not beat the Scarlet Pimpernel! And everything for free; even the gasoline would be paid for by the Germans. I consider it one of the disappointments of my life that after all we were never able to avail ourselves of the new connection. Conditions made it necessary for us to move from Humlebæk on Monday—but I have very often thought of this mechanic with kindness, although I never met him in person.

My acquaintance with the Mexican, however, was renewed in Sweden about twelve months later, and again after the Liberation on several occasions in this country. But that is a pirate story of its own beyond the scope of this narrative.

VI

The House with the Blue Curtains

AFTER the raid on the night of October 1st-2nd, the semidetached house on Buddinge Lane, No. 33A, in Lyngby experienced a change. During the first half of October "the house with the blue curtains," as David called it, became a rapidly growing, hustling and bustling anthill with all sorts of people teeming in and out constantly in the service of Jewish relief. The telephone rang incessantly during the daytime and frequently at night, and during that period our quarterly bill from the telephone company went up from the lowest to the highest rate. Far down the street on either side of Buddinge Lane were cars parked, and the front garden and the neighbor's pavement was crammed with bicycles. By and by we persuaded our colleagues to park their cars on the square in front of the church and in the adjacent street, but apart from that we did nothing or little to hide what happened in the small house. On the con-

120

trary, it was our wish that it should become universally known that here was a travel agency open any time and to anybody who felt impelled to go on a vacation to Sweden. We were well aware of the risk, but we hoped that by the time the Germans got on our heels and closed down the shop we should have finished a useful piece of work.

When we talked on the phone we always exercised a certain amount of caution because of possible wiretapping. We never mentioned Jews, but books, well-known beers like Carlsberg and Tuborg, movie tickets, etc. And that was difficult enough. I remember that one day Sig had a telephone conversation from Buddinge Lane during which he left all his colleagues gaping with admiration because of the confidence with which he juggled with deliveries of scrubbing brushes, buckets, clothes hooks, and so on and so forth. We had never seen such outbursts of imagination and presence of mind. Our admiration changed into hilarity when Sig, who was a wholesale merchant in the hardware business, explained that he had actually been speaking to a business customer.

Our children were in the care of strangers. Special precautionary measures were taken for the sake of the Jews. From the day when the Humlebæk transports started and our own Jewish lodgers disappeared up to the end of the Occupation, no Jew except David entered our house—as far as I know. Both during the work of the group and after its breakdown and the arrest of several of its members, followed by exile for more, I have been reproached because we did not exercise greater circumspection in Lyngby and Humlebæk. Up there it was generally known that at the Hotel Gylfe there was a local center for transport with a main office in Lyngby. But in Humlebæk, too, after the work had been organized all the Jews were placed anywhere but where the group had its quarters, so that a visit by the Gestapo to the Gylfe—and actually they were daily occurrences—would not endanger any of the refugees directly. And that went for Buddinge Lane, too.

Simultaneously with the increasingly large number of Jews seeking evacuation, a corresponding need for assistants sprang up. This was one of the problems which was solved without difficulty. In a way it solved itself. Within a very few days we had—besides our original conspirators from before the raid—a number of young and old Lyngby citizens who placed themselves at our disposal, in many cases giving up all other work. For instance there were Jens Nyskov-Sorensen, Parliamentary usher who was the landlord of my close German-Jewish friend, Professor Berendsohn and his family; Bjarne Sigtryggsson; Mr. Axel Rode, who is now a lecturer at the Academy of Art and who knew the Humlebæk area extremely well from his childhood; a librarian; a midwife, etc.

Mr. Norrild and Professor Prohaska from Sorgenfri were particularly active on the coast together with

122

Sig, Nyskov, and Prior, to put the work in the chaotic days in Humlebæk into more set forms, while the primary object of the others was to take the Jews from their lodgings to the place of embarkation on the beach. We received valuable assistance from my pupils among the students at the State School: Leif Eriksson and Niels Wang, now civil engineers both of them; Anders Thykiær, now an architect; Ole Nielsen, later a naval officer; the tall "Mester," now Doctor Erik Sandoe; Ole Norgaard, the athlete with the nice, kind smile, who as a flight lieutenant in a jet fighter was killed in a crash in West Jutland; Henning Madsen, now a clergyman. Also the Danish-Swiss composer Berg from Rungsted devoted himself entirely to the transport work.

A little later Mr. B. O. Weeke, manufacturer, and Mr. Juel-Christensen, merchant, joined up. It was particularly the work in connection with the subsequent route from Smidstrup which benefited from Weeke's indomitable initiative and optimism and Juel-Christensen's flair for negotiating with the local group—and not least from their good contacts with the sources from which money for the illegal relief work was flowing.

Quite an indispensable force in the work was Dr. Strandbygaard. Many will remember her from those days, in her blue tailored suit, usually with her hands in her pockets and always with a kind and humorous smile. The calmness radiating from her entire person

123

under all circumstances warmed us, and her mere presence was an invigorating tonic for our nerves. Very soon it became an established rule that Dr. Strandbygaard went up to the coast in her car—one of the few using gasoline—to help at the embarkations with her hypodermic syringe and stimulants, accompanied by one or two members of the group who brought the money for the crossing. I think that it was also through Dr. Strandbygaard that I got into contact with Christian Jensen from Husum and Mr. Magius, the engineer from Funen Lane in Lyngby. They became our firm supporters throughout the first half of the month when it was a question of getting saboteurs across in accordance with my promise to send Jews only as passengers for the fishing vessels in Humlebæk. It was an exacting and dangerous job they had taken upon themselves. On the occasions when I met them personally I got the impression that they were made of more robust material than the rest of us. As far as I know they were already participants in the Fight for Freedom, right in the front line. And they also had to pay the price, both of them, and underwent severe torture.

One of the most active among the youngsters was the Orderly. Originally he was a shoemaker—an orthopedic shoemaker. And then he was made an orderly, a higher rank among the sea scouts. As such he had been used to bring messages and orders by sea—with kayak-paddling as his speciality. Now he went around in a taxi and was not cheap. Once we paid one of his bills for a taxi: 800 kroner. All the same I think he was well worth his pay. Twice he was of extraordinary use to us. It was through the Orderly that the police got hold of L. and in that way also recovered the 10,000 kroner out of which he had tricked us. His very association with L. does not seem to indicate any vast knowledge of human nature, which I shall not reproach him for. Indeed, to put it plainly, it was my impression that the Orderly was still in the boy scout stage and that more than anything he considered our work an exciting kind of cross-country race. But he was watchful and alert, and had good connections along the coast.

The day after I had moved the transports from Humlebæk to Smidstrup the Orderly arrived in his taxi at Lyngby to ask for new jobs. I told him that we were working with an organization on the north coast now, and therefore his assistance was not needed any longer, so I thanked him for good companionship. He asked whether he could not possibly be of some further assistance to us, one way or another—he also had certain personal contacts within the Gestapo in Elsinore. "Excellent," I said, "then tell Gestapo-Juhl and his gang that from now on we are really going to do something about the transports from Humlebæk. Tell him that from now on we shall send them out day and night, and that if they concentrate on Humlebæk they will be sure to get a good

125

catch." That was the job for the Orderly. His blue eyes beamed and his whole short, stocky figure expressed an adventurous sense of responsibility. I know nothing further about his activity, but one thing is beyond doubt, and that is that during our crossings from Smidstrup we saw nothing of the pale-green men from Elsinore. This was very likely because of their "full employment" at Humlebæk, thanks to the Orderly's information. Later on he was caught by the Germans. He was sentenced to death, but reprieved at the eleventh hour. He is still a young man, but the torture he suffered has marked him for life.

An experience quite out of the ordinary was ours with Grethe in the Wood, the owner of a hotel and a restaurant in the neighborhood. I looked her up one Sunday morning in the beginning of October. I had heard that she was hiding Jews.

As soon as one got inside one understood that the Germans were not welcome guests here. Everywhere there were small signs on the door to the kitchen, the back room, and to other places "out of bounds" to the guests, and they all said, *Zutritt verboten* (no admittance). I met Grethe in her pretty apartment above the restaurant. She was wearing well-creased slacks with deep pockets in which she buried her hands right up to the elbows, a modish long sweater and short blond hair, framing her cheerful young face. Her cocktail was good and strong, mixed with her customary sense for effects, like herself.

We started talking business at once. Grethe had no more Jews in stock. The hotel had turned out to be rather inadequate for storage purposes. A couple of days ago there had been a raid by a great number of the Gestapo. They had surrounded the house and acted in a very angry manner. Six of them danced a war dance round Grethe with their pistols loaded and pointed at her: "Hands up!"

Grethe put her hands up.

"We know that you are hiding some of these god-damn Jews. There's no use denying it. Where are they?"

Grethe denied it. I also think that she asked them to go to hell. At any rate the Germans got mad.

"Tell us where they are, tell us. Now, right away. And voluntarily. We have means to force you, you know!"

Grethe knew nothing about the Jews at all.

"You are lying. It will cost you dear if we have to find them ourselves. Don't forget that!"

Grethe had nothing to forget.

Then the search began, carried out with proper German thoroughness. First the basement, and then up through the house. The smallest of the Gestapo men even forced his way through the furnace ducts and flues in the walls without finding even one tiny little Jew. When they reached the top floor, where the staff lived, Grethe was ordered to summon all the servants. There was only one missing, a maid, who had gone up to town and had not left the key to her room behind. Grethe knew that, but not the Germans. She placed herself in the narrow corridor in front of the door to the maid's room, and she made her slender body as broad as possible, spreading out both her arms and shouting, "The German police suspect us of hiding Jews. Open your doors."

The doors flew open, and the Germans teemed in on both sides of Grethe—and found nothing. There was nothing strange about that: the eight Jews were in the maid's room behind the door which Grethe covered with her body.

Of course, the Germans were stupid, but while Grethe was telling me the story I must admit that I understood why—in this case. When now and then Grethe stopped pacing the floor and turned her burning eyes like pistol muzzles toward me, I found it almost a matter of course that the zealous Gestapo men had been too busy staring at Grethe to perceive the door behind her.

The angry men had to leave without having solved the riddle, and they did so swearing and threatening. The same night the Jews were removed, and the following day the Germans were back again, and behaved very unpleasantly. Grethe probably was not any the better herself. I do not remember having met anybody who to such a degree radiated scorn at the

Nazis' atrocities against the Jews as did Grethe in the Wood. She was especially angry at Hitler. When she talked about him her eyes emitted sparks like a Leyden Jar. "A bloody nuisance, Mr. Bertelsen, bloody nuisance. He's worse than the devil. But do you know how we shall get rid of him, the monster? He does not deserve to die like other people. I have thought a lot about it, and I have found the method. Do you want to hear it? You know those slicing machines, don't you? We'll put him in a meat-slicing machine. We'll cut him in slices as thin as tissue paper. Damn it but we will. That'll serve him right!"

I visited Grethe a couple of years later together with my wife, I think that it was in the year of the Liberation, one late evening in December. She was then the owner of a very second-class hotel, and during our conversation she was sitting in the large, ugly kitchen making Christmas decorations for the restaurant. She looked twenty years older. The kick of her cocktails had gone. Left behind was a tired, and somewhat diffident and lonely little woman.

"I don't understand it, things after the Liberation, I mean. Do you, Gerda? Or can you explain it to me, Mr. Bertelsen? Soon after the Gestapo's visit I had to go underground and leave the hotel. For a while I lived in an apartment here in Copenhagen and had sort of a boardinghouse for saboteurs and other illegals. Some of them were shot—I shall never forget when they came back carrying Leif Schonemann. A couple of others were tortured. That was worse. You know the nail business and that kind of things. Or they died in Germany. In the end the Germans found my apartment. They forced the door open—fortunately we were not at home—and smashed everything to pieces. They did not leave a splinter. I have now tried to work up a business here. But I am only allowed four pounds of meat a month. And that does not go very far if one has got to live on selling open sandwiches. Then I started buying in the black market—like everybody else. Then someone notified the police, and they gave me thirty days in the lockup. Thirty days!"

Grethe did not understand that the strong arm of the law hits, and must hit, anybody who transgresses its limits. Fighting for freedom and making open sandwiches are two different things. I don't think that I tried to explain this obvious matter to Grethe. I am not sure that I understood it myself—at that time. On the contrary, I think that I found Grethe's reaction a very reasonable one.

"The night before I was going to jail I thought that I had better do something unusual. I decided to get high as a kite—so high that it would last all through my time behind the bars—thirty days! And then I drank till I got so plastered and cockeyed that I couldn't bark or bay, and they had to carry me into the car and from there to the cell. What else could I do? I don't understand it at all. Do you?"

In those days there were many besides Grethe who did not understand. Would it have violated the sense of justice of the Danish people if Grethe had been pardoned, considering her record during the Occupation? Or is this an instance of the right of a supreme authority to retaliate? She who had thought so much evil of Hitler! He died the death of a hero (to some) in an air-raid shelter in Berlin, and in a sense Grethe ended up in a slicing machine. *Denn all Schuld rächt sich auf Erden.* Poor Grethe. . . .

Even after the Lyngby Group had started its own route, we continued our connections with other organizations, most frequently by taking over some of their passengers, or vice versa. Similarly there was a kind of economic exchange. As I have already mentioned, there were especially close relations between us and Professor Ege and his wife, but during a certain period we also sent some of our "clients" through the doctors at the Municipal Hospital and the Bispebjerg Hospital to Sweden. From the very first days of October I remember that I was in contact with Mr. Thorvald Madsen, the manager, and Mrs. Else Zeuthen to ask them to take over some of the Jews who had registered at Lyngby. Dr. Gersfelt from Snekkersten and the Student Group from Regensen, too, were good colleagues in our common cause.

Simultaneously with the organization of the crossings from the coast the system at Buddinge Lane was put in working condition. As soon as we received a message from the people at the places of embarkation about the time of embarkation and number of passengers that could be taken across, we phoned the hosts who were sheltering Jews and told them when to be ready to have their guests picked up by our cars and assistants. The usual rule was that Jews who had their homes in Copenhagen and neighborhood remained in their hiding places, whereas Jews from the provinces were billeted on families in Lyngby until the departure for the coast. All the guest rooms and sofas in Lyngby were more than crowded, and there are many who remember the quiet cordiality of gentle housewives and their hospitality in those days.

Most of the people who passed through Buddinge Lane in October 1943 must have been aware of what was going on behind the blue curtains, and everybody with even the slightest connection with the work in there knew that my wife was the center around which we all gathered. No narrative of the activities of the Lyngby Group could possibly exclude her contribution. Surrounded by her staff of co-workers, always numbering around half a dozen, she ran all the different departments of the operation with firmness. It was of course for reasons of safety necessary to do without written notes or records whenever possible. But when we had to have them—the absolute minimum—they were placed in the most peculiar places, for instance in the margin of one of the volumes of Goethe's collected works. This did not make the task easier.

I know many of those who saw my wife at work at this time were surprised. It is very likely that several of them noticed that as the days and nights passed by, usually without leaving her more than a couple of hours of continuous sleep, she grew thinner and had little dark circles under her eyes. In those days her home was in effect a corridor. All kinds of people brought messages to her, or were sent on special missions by her; every now and then the telephone rang, and she was the only one who was able to answer it fully as she was the only one fully informed. But I believe that nobody ever saw her abandon her attitude of unimpressed calmness and kindness, and that she hardly ever mixed up a name, a telephone number, or an address—where any mistake could be a matter of life and death.

A special problem was to get hold of a sufficient number of cars with drivers on whom we could really depend. Here we were well supported by a list, supplied by one of our assistant groups in Copenhagen, which enumerated both the people we could trust and those we could not. We added other numbers and names as we gained experience, and then it usually covered our needs. In each car that went up to the coast there was always one member of our group if the passengers were Jews. If they were saboteurs—

and only in those cases—were the drivers allowed to drive without being accompanied by one of the group members. This work, which of course was particularly dangerous, was entrusted to a few selected drivers, especially Solje from Lyngby, and Kjeldsen from Copenhagen. Solje was known by many in the group even before the transports. He became our most trusted driver, one hundred per cent safe and reliable, always ready and willing at any time, day and night. Kjeldsen first became attached to the group by accident, but he soon became indispensable. Like Solje he continued, after the persecution of the Jews had stopped, to participate in illegal transports right up to the Liberation.

I consider Kjeldsen the ideal Copenhagen taxi driver. I met him for the first time one day when I had gone up to town to collect contributions for future transports. During the first busy week, it was. It was difficult to get hold of a taxi, and when finally I succeeded the driver said that he could be at my disposal for about three-quarters of an hour. "That will do," I said, and asked him to drive to Slotsholmen where I was going to meet some civil servants from a government ministry. When I got back into the taxi I said rather briefly, "And then to Lyngby."

The effect of these simple words was almost explosive. The short stout man with the kind, round, rubicund face burst into violent protests, expressed in terms which were in very bad harmony with the formal surroundings of the chancellery.

"Absolutely impossible. You'll have to get another car. Didn't I tell you that I could drive for you three-quarters of an hour, and not a minute more? Half an hour has already gone, and you damn well ought to realize that I can't get to Lyngby and back again in a quarter of an hour."

I was in a hurry, and the chances of getting another cab were very small. For a moment I did not know what to do. Then I decided to jump into the car and slam the door behind me, shouting to the angry driver, "Shut up and step on it. This is a question of many human lives."

"That's O.K.," said Kjeldsen in quite a different tone. "Now I know what it's all about, and from now on you can dispose of me two hundred per cent, night and day! Yes, you're right. It's a goddamn mess those crooks in green uniform are making these days. I don't know much about Jews, but this is bloody well against my religion and my morals—hunting people as if thcy were rats. You don't know what I have seen these last days!"

And then he began to tell me what he had experienced while driving Jews to the boats. When the babies began to cry their parents had been forced to silence them by strangling them with one hand until they fainted, and when they regained consciousness, they had to do it over again sometimes.

135

As soon as we got to Lyngby Kjeldsen's name was entered on our list of drivers by my wife—and the name was underlined, for mutual use and satisfaction as long as the group existed. One episode may illustrate both our way of working together and what the man was like.

One day I was informed that a young workman from Soborg, who was very much wanted by the Germans for sabotage, must be shipped to Sweden. He had hidden himself in a gas tank near the main street, and was very nervous, both for himself and also because of his wife who was a Jew and who still lived in Soborg with their baby. I sent one of our group with a car to pick up the wife and the baby, and then I sent for Kjeldsen. He came at once, and I explained to him that this was a saboteur case, and that he had to go on his own to pick up the man at the gas tank, disarm him if he carried a gun, and bring him to the boat at Smidstrup.

"That's O.K.," said Kjeldsen, "I'll see to that. Easy job." And he did.

I was at the embarkation site myself when they arrived shortly before the last rowboat went out to the ship. It was in the evening, and in the darkness I saw a slender, blond young man, somewhat pale and exhausted, but grateful and touched because he had been helped thus far.

"Now, get in that boat there," I said to him, "and when you get on board the ship out there you will meet a young woman and a little girl whom I think you will be glad to see."

He could not help crying. Kjeldsen and I, too, were happy, but we had to hurry off. In those days there was a curfew from 8 P.M. and Kjeldsen's car, driven by charcoal gas, was not exactly a speedster. Professor Ege was up there that night with one of their transports and as they had a gasoline-driven car I drove with them and other members to the Bellevue where we intended to pass the night. We arrived at the hotel in time, and Kjeldsen some minutes past eight.

"Well, looks as if you've had it, Kjeldsen," we told him, "there is a curfew on, you know. How will you get home tonight?"

All of a sudden Kjeldsen's round face turned oblong and sheepish: "Curfew? Curfew? What's that? I never heard of it. I'm stupid—I only went to Bronshoj municipal school. What would I know about any curfew?" And off he went into Copenhagen after curfew.

Professor Ege has told me that Kjeldsen became their most trusted driver during the illegal transports before the Liberation. I have not met him since the Jewish relief operations, but since that night the municipal school in Bronshoj has ranked very high in my opinion among the schools of Greater Copenhagen.

Of other Copenhagen members of the group in

137

Lyngby who joined us by accident, Larking deserves special mention: Speedy Larking, originally an acrobat, now after a fall from the trapeze a performer with the mouth organ as his specialty, plus an act featuring rotating plates and some improbable card tricks. Furthermore, he kept a shop for musical instruments and second-hand goods. I met him on one of the first days of October at Prior's. He had been asked by Mr. Katzenstein to come and help him arrange some things in connection with the family's forthcoming escape to Sweden. Without knowing anything about this small kind man, who introduced himself courteously: "Larking. A pleasure," I immediately accepted his offer of help at the transports, proposed when we were walking to the station on our way home. Any man willing to be entrusted with taking care of all the belongings of a Jewish father with fourteen children should be accepted right away.

Larking was specially useful to us in two ways. He sold the property mentioned earlier for a couple of Jewish families at their request, and he helped us in another way which to us was almost as important as money. We very soon found out that if a man had to work hard for days, frequently without sleep and regular meals, stimulants were a necessity. From the very start of the transport work I had received an offer from a druggist to supply free of charge any amount or kind of medicine, sleeping pills, benzedrine, etc., we might need. Of course we accepted with thanks. In that way Dr. Strandbygaard got all she needed for the Jews before the crossings. The rest of us were mostly interested in the stimulants, the so-called "pep pills," and we also received ample supplies of sleeping pills when we had difficulty in getting the sleep which was so necessary under the prevailing tense conditions. But unfortunately the drugstore did not sell tobacco, and to many of the young people, both at Humlebæk and Lyngby, cigarettes were under these circumstances almost a necessity of life. From other quarters I have learned that the big tobacco manufacturers placed themselves at the disposal of the transport groups. In Lyngby we did not know anything about that and had to satisfy our requirements beyond the scanty, personal rations in other ways. This is where Larking proved useful again. Through special channels he supplied us with large quantities of cigarettes and tobacco bought on the black market for 2,300 kroner in all. The black marketeer was an SS man. The price was exorbitant, the quality bad, but the effect surprising. This was the only time that I bought goods on the black market or traded with the Germans in Denmark— and then it was through an intermediary! But I have rarely spent money for a more useful purpose. The members of the group who were suffering from fatigue and the agonies of frustrated tobacco addiction were soon revived by the magic and soothing herb, and our supplies were so ample that we were even

139

able to let our colleagues from other organizations share our abundance. Later on, after the breakup of the Lyngby Group, when I arrived in Sweden I offered some of the oldest pupils from the Danish school in Lund some cigarettes from the black-market packets I had brought with me. When they had taken one puff my gift was rejected as absolutely unsmokable. In a neutral country they were used to better quality tobacco. The pleasures of life as well as its agonies are subject to the law of relativity, I realized.

By far the majority of the Danish Jews live in or around Copenhagen nowadays. But the few who lived in the provinces were exposed to dangers of the same nature and strength during the persecutions. Some of them went up to the capital and got to Sweden along with their Copenhagen fellow sufferers, but others, who had no connection with transport groups, were often in an extremely precarious situation. As soon as the transports began to be relieved of the sudden and violent flow from the capital it became our task to look for Jews in the rest of the country, if there were any left. So we started organizing a search, to be as country-wide as possible, and began on Zealand.

We heard rumors of a group of Jews from northwestern Zealand that had made an unsuccessful attempt to escape from Ods Herred, and who had been in difficulties ever since. I phoned to Uffe Grosen, a high school principal, on Zealand. He was supposed to know about the matter, and we arranged that he should meet me in Lyngby to discuss the details. Grosen proved to be the man needed both by the Jews and by our group. The day after our conversation he arrived with an overcrowded bus—and 5,000 kroner to pay for the tickets. Because of our usual precautionary measures, the passengers were not taken to Buddinge Lane, but after a meal at Mr. Bo's in Christian Winther's Road they were transferred to taxis which took them direct to the "ferry."

In the same way we learned about some Jews at Vordingborg who had tried to escape, but in vain. We had no concrete information at all—and no contacts in that town. Nevertheless our member Kleener went down there to find out if help was needed. Herman Kleener was a student at the faculty of humanities, and had nearly finished his studies. He was one of my former pupils from the high school in Jutland. I met him by accident one day when I was driving down Frederiksberg Avenue. I hailed him, and as there was no time for negotiations on the spot he left his bike against a tree and jumped into the taxi. From that moment he was one of the group, and he charged at all the tasks given him with almost suicidal ardor. And he was given some pretty difficult ones!

Kleener succeeded in contacting the Vordingborg Jews and bringing them right across the island of

Zealand and up to the boat at Smidstrup beach, a piece of work worthy of the best intelligence agents. This achievement almost equaled his famous search for the present librarian at the Mosaic Religious Community, Julius Margolinsky. It was David's idea that we should try to get hold of Margolinsky. Perhaps in that way we might get some names and addresses of Jews who had not yet had a chance to escape. Before the search started we knew nothing about the librarian's whrereabouts except that he was somewhere in Denmark. Kleener got on his track and followed it from one place to another. A very difficult job, as the librarian was wanted by the Germans and was traveling disguised, under false names, sometimes with and sometimes without a beard. Finally he found him gone underground at the Dianalund Sanatorium.

It was also through David that I got information about the so-called *chaluzim*. They were the young foreign pioneers of both sexes who before the war were being trained in Denmark as farmers with a view to future emigration to Palestine. There were about four hundred of them scattered all over the country. (Incidentally, Margolinsky had organized this kind of work.) A well-known man from a district in Jutland where we thought there must be many chaluzims declared that he was completely unaware of the existence of Jews in his district, and consequently he was unable to help us. So I had to send a member of the group over there to investigate the matter. The result was that some time later the organization was able to "export" quite a large number of these Jewish farmers. It is to be hoped that they have subsequently been able to begin their careers in the new Israel.

Jews are not commonly employed in agricultural work in Denmark. I remember one incident which led to a very interesting discussion with a West Jutland small holder, who was a Jew. I met him in his lodging at Mrs. Finsen's on Lyngby Farm the same day we shipped him across to Sweden. He was from Jutland, and his name was David Hudan, a graduate of Viborg College. After the Liberation he became the author of an autobiographical novel: *From Haifa to Hammerum Herred,* a thorough and very well-written narrative based on the psychological tension between the Jew and the Jutlander. In my opinion it ranks with the best descriptions of Jews in our literature.

Mr. Thiesen was a teacher and our neighbor in Buddinge Lane, who helped the group greatly by placing his telephone at our disposal for conversations which must under no circumstances be overheard. Through him we heard that at Ryomgaard in Jutland there was a Jewish woman who was ill and broken in body and mind by worries about herself and her relatives. She was fetched by train, and after

143

one day's stop at Mrs. Hemmingsen's in Buddinge Lane was sent across on one of Professor Ege's transports.

Among our most prominent passengers from the provinces was a prisoner from the State Prison at Horsens, Jutland. One day we received an application from Horsens requesting us to take care of one of the two Jewish prisoners of the State Prison. He had not yet served his term in full, but he had won the sympathy of the staff to such an extent that they now wanted to safeguard him against any possibility that the Germans might get the idea of searching Danish prisons as they had searched our hospitals. The man from Horsens was received with open arms together with his attendant, a Jewish warder, by Niels Andersen in his apartment at Ulrikkenborg Square. I hope that later on in Sweden he appreciated the service of both Horsens and Lyngby.

It is still miraculous to me that we had no losses of life at all during the trips to the coast or during the crossings to Sweden. It is true that we never let the cars drive in convoy or immediately after one another, and that we saw to it that the traffic was routed along as many different roads as possible. But on the days of big transports it could not be avoided that the traffic between Lyngby and Humlebæk must have seemed abnormal. Something very nearly went wrong twice on the same day and in the same place. When one of our cars with Mr. Bruné from Virum as the

144

guide was driving down the road from Horsholm it was stopped by a German sentry.

"Who are you?" he asked.

Bruné told him his name.

"Who is that?" The German pointed at one of the passengers in the back seat.

"His name is Soren Kirkegaard."

"Where are you going?"

"To a birthday party at Aunt Malene's in Usserod."

"Bitte fahren," said the sentry.

Whereupon Bruné continued the trip to Aunt Malene's imaginary party. . . .

Later on that afternoon the Germans stopped another car, guided by Big P.—a medical student, Bent Petersen, a blond rock of calmness, balance, and good humor. (He died, alas, during his resistance work at a Jutland hospital.) This time the Germans demanded that they should get out to be examined. Petersen made objections, but in vain. Then he tried to show them a 500-kroner note. It was angrily rejected.

"Alle aussteigen! Schnell!"

Then something happened which probably ought to be a note in the margin of the German list of sins in Denmark. Big P. turned round and pointed at some small dark heads in the back of the car.

"Seien Sie doch Menschen. Wir haben ja Kinder mit!" (Be human. We have children with us!)

The German had a look at them, then slammed the door. *"Weiter fahren!"*

In the beginning it was almost exclusively those entirely of Jewish blood and saboteurs who were sent to Sweden. Later on there were also some part Jews. Rumor had it that the meager results of the first persecutions had roused Hitler's fury, and that the Germans intended to increase its scope. Consequently we got many applications from part Jews, and I went up to see a high-ranking official in the Foreign Ministry. He answered my question by giving me a copy, with the official stamp of the ministry, of the correspondence between Mr. Svenningsen, director of the Foreign Ministry, and Dr. Best concerning the rules of the *Judenaktion* in Denmark (the persecution of Jews in Denmark). Dr. Best referred to the so-called Nürnberg Acts according to which only whole Jews who had not married Aryans came under the proscription. To the letter was added the rather unsatisfactory information that these rules were the ones in force in Denmark *bisher* (so far). Nobody in the ministry wanted to add anything to the contents of the letter, not even the head of the visa office, whom I looked up in his home. He did not think he was in a position to judge whether others than whole Jews could be considered in danger. So I made it a practice, when I was asked by part Jews, to show them a copy of this letter, offering them a crossing if they felt they were in danger. The prospect of many years of exile

146

in Sweden was not always encouraging, but still most preferred it to an existence at home under constant fear of transportation to Germany.

In the course of the first couple of weeks the work at Buddinge Lane increased continuously and became more and more expertly organized. It was a great help to my wife that the difficult problem of food for ourselves and our colleagues was solved by help from outside. As we had no permanent help in the house, we "borrowed" maids from different colleagues until in the end the food was delivered and served by Miss Ulff's Domestic School.

We should probably have continued along these lines indefinitely if I had not received a letter in the middle of the month which made it necessary to alter the methods of work. From a certain course in Sorgenfri, which had proved extremely well informed on several occasions, I received a brief note to the effect that a group of Danish Nazis were searching the homes of all those who had helped Jews, and that by means of torture they were trying to force them to reveal the names and addresses of other organizations. The same night I called on Chief of Police Mouridsen and showed him the letter. He immediately sent some men to patrol the streets outside the house in Buddinge Lane, as well as Norrild's and Prohaska's houses in Sorgenfri. However, we moved the whole headquarters the following day after the police had again—and urgently—requested us to do so. Facing the imminent possibility that a gang of Nazis might bring about the breakdown not only of our, but also of other organizations, I felt that I must discontinue the line we had followed right from the beginning: for the house in Buddinge Lane to be the center of our operations as long as the transports were carried on.

On several occasions Dr. Strandbygaard had suggested that we should move the administration of the organization to her more discreetly situated villa in Caroline Amalie Road. Now I accepted the invitation, and during the last half of the month the group had its headquarters at Dr. Strandbygaard's. The functions and management of the group remained unaltered. My wife and I also moved from Buddinge Lane and spent the nights at the Bellevue Seaside Hotel. As far as we were concerned, the new state of affairs was an improvement, for now we had an opportunity to sleep all the night through without being disturbed. But as far as the expected increased security of the transport work was concerned, the move was probably a rather doubtful improvement. Neither the legendary calmness of our hostess, the matronly care of her assistant Miss Christiansen, nor the beautiful rooms filled with the peaceful purring of the Strandbygaard cats, could cover what was happening in this new setting. While the rest of us were carrying on our business as a travel agency in the sitting room, Miss Strandbygaard would hold

148

meetings with people from the actual resistance movement. Weapons and explosives had been hidden all over her garden and in the house, and on the same sofas where we were sitting the various lodgers in the house—for instance "Olgier the First" and "Olgier the Second," both paratroopers—had been lying only a few days before with their maps and sketches of factories in Copenhagen working for the German war industry. A couple of days later we read in the papers that these factories had been blown up in the middle of the night by saboteurs.

VII

*From the Sound
to the Kattegat*

As MENTIONED several times before, I felt from
the very first night at Humlebæk the heavy pressure
of having the responsibility for a task which I had
taken upon myself although I thought that I lacked
natural qualifications to carry it out. Yet all the same
I had not been able to reject it. Also, once the work
had been properly organized, thanks to my excellent
colleagues, I could not help thinking of the possibility
of finding an organization which could take over our
transport activities and carry them on with less danger for the Jews. But the attempt we made in that
respect proved without result. Some of my assistants,
whom I had sent to Copenhagen to study the transports from the harbor, told me how they had seen
Jews being led to the boat in the middle of the day
through a crowd of spectators, including a number
of German soldiers. That did not sound very safe.

One day I myself went up to town and down to

the southern part of the harbor to talk to the leader of another organization and with the captain of a ship which a few days previously had taken a big transport across, financed by us. The man, a restaurant-keeper, had done a splendid job—I heard that from others too—but the precautions were far behind the Humlebæk route, in my opinion. The Jews all gathered together in the restaurant prior to the embarkation. And even when it was not in the very room where we were sitting now discussing the future and having a cup of coffee, while the table next to us was occupied by soldiers in green, at least it was in the same building and on the same floor. It may have been an easy matter to lead them across the street and the rails down to the ship which was moored right off the restaurant, but when I went on board I felt somewhat shaken at what the captain told me about the latest transport. The ship was carrying brown coal to Poland and Jews to Sweden. The procedure was to hide the Jews forward in the water tank, but the opening leading into it was so small that it could be used as a hiding place for children only—or for very thin young people. How the rest were hidden I do not remember—probably in the bunker hold.

The critical moment came when the German harbor police went on board to check the papers before sailing. On the latest trip they had a narrow escape. Some of the children in the water tank started crying just as the Germans came aboard. Although they had managed to deafen the police by opening the waste-watercocks and starting the winches, I could not help comparing conditions there with those obtaining for our own operation. I did not doubt that I would give the prize to Humlebæk: the remote brick factory on the coast, the out-of-the-way Nivaa pier near it, with plenty of possibilities for shelter among the reeds and bushes in case of a surprise visit during the nightly embarkations. And above all, at Humlebæk we avoided forcing the Germans to make visits to our ships. As far as I know there were never any mishaps in connection with the crossings from Copenhagen, but after my visit to the harbor I realized that if I was to hand over our transport operation to others it would not be to an organization with departures from the capital.

For the time being there was nothing to do but to continue the work, and be on constant lookout for new possibilities. One great encouragement was that Mr. Kampmann, a civil engineer working at the Technical High School, joined the group. He had previously worked for another and bigger organization where the work had been very specialized without any actual responsible leader. He believed that this entailed too much uncertainty as regards the work, and that in this respect the organization of the Lyngby Group was an improvement. I cannot deny that this recognition of our work pleased me very

152

much, and also his support meant a valuable additional increase in the staff. I do not know whether Kampmann was already active in the fight for freedom at that time. Later on, in Sweden, I read that he had been imprisoned after an exchange of shots at his home in Hoje Skodsborg. He was subjected to cruel torture and was among the prisoners locked up in the top floor of Shell House in Copenhagen, and was liberated during the British air attack.

In the morning of October 11 Professor Prohaska phoned me from the Technical High School and asked me to meet him there. He informed me that the night before he had been at Olsen's brick factory when a car from Copenhagen, driven by charcoal gas, had stopped outside the entrance, and a man, who said that he was the head clerk at a Copenhagen steamship company which transported Jews, asked to see Mr. Bertelsen. Prohaska explained that I was not there, and asked him to remove his car, which was parked with the engine running and the fire from the generator burning in the dark, as if to tell the whole world that this was the hiding place of the Jews. They then moved a little bit down the road, and the man from the shipping company told Prohaska that in Copenhagen there were many misgivings about the conditions at Humlebæk. He suggested that the transports should be handed over to another organization, which worked farther south under what they thought were safer conditions.

Prohaska, who knew my views, gave the group's temporary promise to hand over the work to others, and it was arranged that if I agreed the other organization should fetch our Jews the following Monday afternoon. As a matter of fact, this arrangement clashed with our new plans, as we had just arranged with the police and the port authorities to make a departure from the harbor itself. Nevertheless, I agreed to the Copenhagen proposal, mostly because of the increasing interest of the Germans in the Hotel Gylfe and the Nivaa pier and its surroundings, a fact which made the situation ever more difficult and the thought of moving more urgent. So it was with a feeling of relief that after the talk at the High School I drove up to the Gylfe together with Kampmann to wind up the route for good after its exciting career. In the preceding week about six hundred passengers had been carried across the Sound by the Humlebæk route, so it had really fulfilled its obligations. And now it had to go.

The winding up took place the same night—but in quite a different way from what we had expected. Late in the afternoon there arrived at the hotel a car containing three or four young men. They were representatives from the group which was to take over our Jews, and as far as I remember they had a power of attorney with them. Pursuant to our agreement, I paid them nearly all the cash we had left. Shortly afterwards the first of the cars arrived to take the Jews to the new place of embarkation. I asked the driver and the man who was with him where they came from.

"From Copenhagen," he said.

"How many cars can we expect?"

"About twenty."

That was a suitable number. We had sixty-seven Jews living in the brick factory. "Where are you going?"

"To Gjorslev on Stevns."

"Which way are you going?"

"The direct road, down the Promenade through Copenhagen, and down along the coast."

"All of you? One after another?"

"Yes!"

That did not sound right to me. We were used to letting the cars take different routes, and here before my mental eye, I saw a cortège of cars full of Jews driving down the Promenade and on, down the sixty-mile-long route to Stevns, one after the other! If I had felt pleased and relieved, I now sensed the old feeling of uncertainty and unrest return and the responsibility weighed doubly heavy upon me. How could I in common decency leave my Jews to what in my opinion appeared to be such an amateurish and dangerous treatment? But on the other hand, what else was there to do? The agreement was made and the money paid.

In the midst of these desperate considerations a

young man suddenly rushed into the room and demanded to see me. With a frankness which was quite unusual under such conditions he introduced himself: Erik Bennike. He explained briefly that he was lying with a transport off Smidstrup, and he was to leave in an hour and a half. The ship had been paid for and was ready to take all our Jews if we could bring them to the coast at once. It sounded absolutely incredible, yet absolutely convincing at the same time because of the young man's brief and concise report.

One of the popular Jewish beliefs I have met with is that a man can be another man's "angel." The young first lieutenant and civil engineer was such an angel, sent by heaven, or as in classical tragedy, a *deus ex machina*, who solves the tragic conflict when no mortal recourse is left. Right from the moment I met him I did not doubt or hesitate as to what I should do. Seldom or never has a man influenced me so strongly as did Erik Bennike by the force and strength which spontaneously radiated from his personality. His boyish and youthful face with dark vivid eyes, luminous with intelligence and good will, his whole body expressing a concentration of purposeful power and inherent authority, immediately gave me the feeling that here I was facing a personality of unusual dimensions. The book on him published by his friends and associates after his death and descriptions by others who knew him have confirmed the correctness of this impression. There is no doubt, as far as I am concerned, that when Erik Bennike was killed by Gestapo bullets in Nyhavn on April 18, 1945, we lost one of the most potentially important young men of this country.

Bennike's visit to the Gylfe was decisive for the activities of the Lyngby Group during the rest of October. Having notified Villumsen about directing the cars which were expected from Copenhagen to Smidstrup with the Jews from the brick factory, I drove in the car which had just arrived with the young lieutenant to our new place of embarkation on the Kattegat. On the way we stopped outside a house in Humlebæk and picked up a Jewish family consisting of the parents and two grown-up children. Among our many passengers I do not remember having met a family so exhausted and worn out by sufferings and disappointments in connection with their attempts to reach the rescue ship. Since the raid of October 10 they had been to several places on the coast, both on the Sound and on the sea, but without any result, and they had been tricked out of their money without getting help. In Gilleleje they had witnessed the panic when ninety Jews had been caught in the attic of the local church, and literally speaking they had been hunted across country, over fences and barbed wire, in despair bordering on complete hopelessness. They told me that they had taken their poison capsules out twice in order to evade

157

their pursuers, but in both cases the son's proposal to try one more chance had made them give it up at the last minute. When we got to Smidstrup, Bennike took them direct to the boat. Their gratitude at being saved was overwhelming.

On October 11 of every year since that night I have received a bunch of flowers from that family. I have accepted them with pleasure, but in my mind I send them on to Erik Bennike's grave. That day he not only saved that family but, by forming the connection between Lyngby and Smidstrup, he prepared and lightened the road for hundreds more persecuted folk on their way to freedom.

While Bennike was down at the beach I phoned the Gylfe to hear how the dispatch of Jews from the brick factory was going. Villumsen told me that a couple of the Copenhagen cars had arrived, but the drivers referred to their orders from the other organization and were unwilling to come to Smidstrup. Halfway through the conversation we were cut off— which always makes me really desperate! A few minutes afterwards I was phoned by Villumsen. More than half the cars had arrived by then, but there was general confusion and excitement because of the conflicting orders. I asked Villumsen to impress on the Copenhagen men how much was at stake. The ship waiting at Smidstrup could take all our Jews, its departure could be delayed for another hour, and all the Jews could make it in safety if the drivers did

158

their duty. Those who refused to obey my orders would be held responsible for the lives they endangered. Bennike seconded me by fiery words, and Villumsen must both have understood us and repeated our words with all the clearness one could wish for because a moment later he phoned us again to say that now they were on the way with all our guests from Humlebæk.

From that night the Lyngby Group was closely connected with the organization at Smidstrup. When the ship had left for Höganäs—all the cars arrived in time except two, whose passengers were then billeted in some summer cottages and sent across the following day—I had a conversation with the leader of the transports. He described briefly and concisely how the work up there was organized. We agreed on the terms for our working together, and during the rest of the month the small rooms of the leader, Mr. Lassen, became the headquarters of the Lyngby Group just as the Gylfe had been at Humlebæk.

VIII

The Smidstrup Route

IT IS HIGHLY improbable that there were any illegal transport groups which were better organized than the one at Smidstrup. Besides Mr. Lassen, the organization consisted mainly of people from Gilleleje, a teacher at an elementary school, a manufacturer, the local coast guard, a policeman, the ex-district medical officer, Mr. Vilstrup, who has since died, and a few others. Everything was well planned and the whole organization worked with almost mechanical precision and military discipline—it was no mere coincidence that the chief of the transports, Mr. Lassen, was an ex-officer in the army. The new state of affairs was ideal for us. Between the hills and the vast pine plantations there were hundreds of summer cottages, and Lassen had the keys to most of them, so that the Jews could wait there for the arrival of the ship, and if need be sleep there a night or two. For the Gestapo to find among all these houses exactly the ones in which the refugees were hidden was much like finding the proverbial needle in the haystack, and in order to increase the protection against visits by undesired persons, especially from the Gestapo headquarters in Gilleleje, there were guards and signals on the road between Smidstrup and Gilleleje. They informed Lassen and his colleagues of anything that looked suspicious.

Fixed agreements had been made with the fishermen and the skippers in Gilleleje as to prices and procedure. When the time for embarkation was almost at hand and the droning sound of the ship's engines came closer from the east, the passengers were swiftly brought from their lodgings in the summer cottages through the plantation down to the edge of the rather narrow beach. Here, too, they were excellently covered. Even a keen observer would have difficulty in discerning human silhouettes in the darkness under the trees, even were he only a few paces away.

Making connections with the ship was Lassen's job. From one of the hilltops he would use his torch to show the skipper, still out at sea, where the landing place was. Otherwise the use of fire and light was prohibited, and all conversation was in a whisper. As soon as the ship dropped anchor the Jews were led across the beach and down to the small pier or breakwater, and from there taken out in rowboats to the waiting ship. Just as everywhere that work of this kind was carried out, these minutes were the really critical ones, but thanks to the speed and the precision of the transfer, and the precautionary measures, the transports were always carried out comfortably, and I do not recall any instances when the nervousness of our passengers was perceptible.

The Lyngby Group's transfer to the Smidstrup area meant figuratively that finally it had got into smooth waters after the tempestuous, nerve-racking days at Humlebæk. Every time I think back, those nights on the north coast of Zealand appear before me in a strange, solemn, inexplicable radiance. It was as if the nature of the beach, the dark sky, and the sea with its unbelievably powerful phosphorescence around the boats and the oars, as they rowed toward the ship, combined miraculously, framing the picture and symbolizing the sentiments which penetrated the lives of many Danes in the days of the persecutions of the Jews. Radiant light over a pitch-black sea!

I remember particularly one night late in October. We were walking along the beach after having sent the last boat off to the ship. The sky was overcast with heavy clouds, but the phosphorescence formed a luminous edge along the coast. The work and the tension were things of the past. Only our steps on the beach and the dull humming of the ships' engines broke the silence. For fourteen days in succession we had shared the same experience, but nevertheless the finished embarkation filled our souls each time with this peculiar, almost too intense feeling of happiness, which seemed to me to be entirely different from all other emotional experiences. I was walking beside Dr. Strandbygaard. Suddenly she said, "Isn't this strange? Don't you think so? A very strange feeling! It's almost like experiencing again the overwhelming love of one's youth."

People from other parts of the coast had the same impression. One night when as usual a couple of us were walking up from the beach at Humlebæk, the work finished, there was a silence. Everybody was absorbed in his own thoughts. There was only the humming sound of the engines gradually disappearing toward the Swedish coast.

All of a sudden Larking said, "Do you know what I think I am feeling, Mr. Bertelsen?" Larking was always very careful to observe all the formalities.

"Perhaps, but tell me anyway, Larking."

"I feel—hang it—I feel like throwing myself down upon the road, and saying thank you!"

I hope that if Larking reads this he will forgive me my breach of confidence. But I am sure, my dear friend, that that night you said something very essential.

My wife participated only once in an embarkation. Bound as she was night and day by the hard toil in the "office" in Lyngby, she allowed herself only this one evening toward the end of October to accompany me to Smidstrup. Otherwise she did not get outside the house very often, much against her nature and custom. But the whole atmosphere of the beach up there rested like a blessing on the relief work, and on the rooms in Buddinge Lane. One day, after the transports had ended and the group had been dissolved, and we had gone underground on Stevns, we were walking with our children down the road along the cliff. As usual we were talking about the events of the last month and about the prospects of the immediate future. We agreed that no matter what might happen to us we could not have done without that period.

"No, because it's like this," said Gerda very quietly, "it's as if we never realized before what it means to live."

I was struck by surprise and it was impossible for me to answer. Besides, the statement needed no answer. My wife has a rich emotional nature, but is absolutely devoid of sentimentality. She is the Enemy No. 1 of clichés and trite phrases. But her words that day seemed to me the most moving interpretation I know of the deep and eternally valid truth which Schiller immortalized in his famous lines: *Und setzet Ihr nicht das Leben ein, nie wird Euch das Leben gewonnen sein.* (Life will not be worth living if one does not stake it.)

But it is not my intention to analyze sentiments and emotions here, only to try to recall them. I want to set down a couple of distinctive incidents which I

164

remember as evidencing the feelings that moved the Jews amid their escape.

I am glad to mention one of them, since it is connected with my wife's only visit to the coast—the one I just mentioned—on one of the last nights of the transports. I was sitting in one of the summer cottages, which served as a temporary hiding place for our passengers, talking to an elderly married couple. They were superior cultured German Jews whom I had known before the escape. It was just before sunset, but the room was dark behind the blacked-out windows. It was out of the question to put on any light. Then the door was opened all of a sudden and Gerda entered. I saw her form like a silhouette with the glowing western sky as background. For some reason or other it made a very deep impression on me.

Later on I met the same refugees in Sweden. They told me that that very night they had decided that they would themselves put an end to the persecution. In Germany they had been scoffed at, threatened, tortured. In the end their property had been seized and they had been hunted almost to death. After the escape to Denmark they had hoped that they could settle down and live there in peace, at any rate till the war was over. And now the persecutions were beginning again. "We talked the matter over, just before you joined us," said the old gentleman, "and we had agreed that this was the limit. We could not

165

go on. We did not want to flee to a strange country, away from the hangmen of our people. We considered it both unworthy and insuperable. We had our poison pills and had both of us decided to use them. Then your young, beautiful wife entered. It was as if the sun came through the door into the room to us. From that moment all thoughts of suicide left us completely."

A young Jewess, also a German refugee, told me after our homecoming from Sweden that she, too, had been among our passengers from Smidstrup. Before that she had lived for a few terrible days in Gilleleje at the time when a large number of refugees were caught by the Gestapo in the local church, and others at the harbor. She was very young, almost a child. And the horrors of those days had left only a dull chaotic memory. But then she suddenly remembered herself on board a ship together with one hundred fifty fellow passengers. The thing she would never forget was what happened when they got nearer to the Swedish coast. The skipper had ordered dead silence during the crossing. But the very moment it was announced that they were passing the three-mile limit and were in Swedish territorial waters, all the passengers began singing, and Israel's ancient paean: *Sjema Yisroel* sounded powerfully, rolling jubilantly toward the Swedish coast and back to the beaches of Denmark as they disappeared behind them.

166

Miss F. told me that during her childhood and youth she had had no contact with the Jewish religion. She belonged to an assimilated German-Jewish family, and she did not become a believer in the orthodox sense of the word at a later stage. But from that moment on the ship in the Kattegat between Denmark and Sweden she had felt and understood that her soul had deep roots not only among the Jewish people, but also in the Jewish faith.

Our collaboration with Smidstrup lasted until the Lyngby Group was dissolved.

During the last week the demand for transports was decreasing, but we still had a big or a small boat going across to Höganäs every night. Gradually there was a proportional increase in the number of half Jews and illegals, and as far as I could see a remarkably large number of blind, deaf and dumb, infirm, and in other ways invalid whole Jews. In the end the route worked almost as regularly as an ordinary tourist line with a fixed schedule. I hope that it continued long after we from Lyngby had to go underground and had lost contact with it. I resumed the connection with Mr. Lassen later on in Sweden when I received a Christmas card from the Danish Brigade. He, too, had in the end been compelled to make the crossing as a passenger. He and his helpers deserve a special chapter in the history of the illegal traffic.

IX

The Breakdown

THE ACTIVITIES of the Lyngby Group lasted altogether for a period of one month. Then they broke down. It is only remarkable, really, that it did not happen long before considering the fact that in Buddinge Lane we had worked so openly, in fact right under the eyes of the public.

The reason for the breakdown was the traditional one: an informer. One day toward the end of October a man came to see Villumsen, via an intermediary, at the Hotel Gylfe. He asked to get a connection to Sweden. He was a saboteur, and had to escape. Villumsen, who did not trust the man, sent for Bjarne Sigtryggsson, who had by then returned to his work and his house in Lyngby, and the two of them questioned the man. He was about forty, rather tall, slender, with a small head and regular features, rather well dressed. Asked if he was armed, he produced a revolver. Had he any money for the crossing? Yes, he was able to pay 10,000 kroner. That was quite a big amount and in itself enough to make them suspicious, but from the days of the transports they were used to big figures, and the two saw their chance of getting money to pay the 8,000 kroner we still owed the fisherman who had not been paid the whole of the amount he had been promised for his help on the "Big Transport."

The time for the crossing was arranged, and on the evening of October 28 a fisherman brought his ship alongside the pier off the Gylfe to pick up the saboteur. Another couple of illegals, who had come up there to try to get across, were allowed on board free of charge. As the supposed saboteur, who in reality was Paul Hennig, the Gestapo and Danish-German leader of the persecution of the Jews, was walking down toward the boat he suddenly took out his torch and signaled. Some Gestapo men who had hidden themselves near by immediately started shooting at Villumsen and Sig and their helpers, who were assembled outside the hotel. When the fisherman heard the shooting he quickly let go the hawser. He managed to get himself and his two passengers safely across to Sweden. Villumsen and a couple of the others got caught, but Sig got round the house and behind the adjoining hill, still with bullets whizzing past his ears. He felt that he was being pursued and ran for his life, and when he had used all his strength he threw himself into the bushes along the road.

The next day Sig told me that he had never in his

life been so scared. Still, he had enough presence of mind, when he had caught his breath, to go back to town, change his clothes and put on some belonging to a friend of his. Then with his hands in his pockets and a cap pulled down over his eyes he sauntered down to Olsen at the brick factory. He was received with open arms, but as—since the days of the big transports—the Gestapo kept an eye on him he at once phoned the Danish police at Krogerup and asked them to come and pick up a suspicious-looking person. The Danish police took Sig to the palace in triumph, and there he was entertained as if he were a feudal lord. But Krogerup, too, was the object of the Germans' suspicion, so even there he could not feel safe. After a good night's sleep in the police station he went down to the coast again and got his clothes back, except his hat which had fallen off when he fled from the German bullets, and then he went by train to Copenhagen, and bought a fine new hat at the English House department store.

The same night there was a raid on Sig's parents' house in Lyngby. The two leaders, on the Gestapo side, of the nocturnal drama in Humlebæk, Paul Hennig and criminal inspector Renner, cross-examined Mr. Sigtryggsson senior and his wife while they were still in bed, and showed them the revolvers with which they had shot at their son, and guaranteed that even if they had missed him this time they would not the next time if he continued his criminal activities. They knew that he was a member of an illegal group, and in that connection they asked if Mr. Sigtryggsson knew a "Professor Prosa," or something of the sort.

When Mr. Sigtryggsson, my headmaster, told me about this in the morning when we met in school, where I had just resumed my work after the October vacation, I went straight up to the Technical High School and asked the janitor to get hold of Professor Prohaska, who was giving a lecture. I told the Professor that he was wanted by the Gestapo, and added that if he wished he could get across from Smidstrup the same night. The Professor made up his mind at once: he wanted to wait and see for a little while and go underground with his family. He made a wise decision. Later, when the persecution of the Jews had stopped completely and the Germans had other things on their minds, he was able to return to his home and continue his work at the High School without any hindrance.

From the Technical High School I went straight up to the Bellevue where I met my wife, together with Professor and Mrs. Ege and their helpers. Like us they had spent the night in the hotel after the transport from Smidstrup the night before. I told them what had happened, and then went straight home to Buddinge Lane, expecting Sig to look me up there. He did so shortly after my return. Sig was still somewhat shocked at what had taken place dur-

171

ing the night, and asked me very urgently to give it up while there was still time to do so. "Neither you nor I have nerves to work under the conditions now prevailing on the coast. Last night I learned that it takes people with nerves of steel when guns come into the picture."

I had to admit that, I, too, was no hero when the guns began to blaze. I remembered a visit to the police station in Lyngby at the beginning of the transports. It was the day after young Heilesen had been shot in Taarbæk harbor while helping Jews in the boats. He was the son of a well-known supreme court attorney. The police showed me the bullets they had found, and some pictures of the young man, closeups of him lying on the bridge, his head blown to pieces. I am not hardened against sights of this kind, and the police pictures touched me deeply. Also, I could not help thinking of our own work in Lyngby. It was not, however, the personal danger in connection with the transports that was of great significance to us when the group and I planned and arranged the work. There was only one exception: when it was a question of transporting saboteurs. In such cases, as I have already stated, it was necessary to take certain measures to protect those who helped in the transport.

In their proclamation of August 29 the Germans had threatened death sentences for that kind of crime. As far as the Jew Transports were concerned, the personal danger was completely overshadowed by the risk that something might go wrong because we were not carrying out the job properly. And also because under those circumstances I was convinced that we should not use the means which were used so brutally and ruthlessly by our opponents.

One night when I was driving with Norrild up to Humlebæk we discussed this last problem. Norrild then reminded me that the same day we had had an offer from some groups of the organization "Free Danes" to escort our transports with armed groups to protect the trucks from being captured by the Gestapo.

I told him that I had thought the matter over, but that I felt we ought to say no, thank you. It was obvious that it was only the Gestapo who had been put on the job, and they were numerically too few. But if we, on our part, started using guns up and down the coast there was the possibility that the Germans might put the *Wehrmacht* on the job to stop the whole business, and there was no doubt that they could do so if they wanted to.

Much to my surprise Norrild bent toward me and said with a smile, "I do not disagree. But, my dear Bertelsen! What has happened to you, a convinced pacifist?"

He hit the bull's-eye there. It was almost like a sign from heaven. Since my earliest boyhood I had been a pacifist. Although I was not a member, I once wrote for the organ of the movement *Never Another War* an article in which I stood aloof from any kind of violence, even in defense. That was one of the few points where I had been absolutely in disagreement with my friend and professional colleague. And now it struck me, all of a sudden, that in answering his question and in thinking the matter out I had not taken my earlier theories into consideration even for one second. My conclusion was based exclusively on the question of whether in the present situation it would be advisable and expedient to kill the Germans and their helpers. I shall remember this talk as long as I live. It proved to me, like a revelation, to what extent we are directed by our experiences and the topical situations in which life places us, and not by abstract theory.

I have also had a chance since then to confirm the very important experience of that night. A month later when one of my colleagues visited me underground, I gave him the description of the informer from Humlebæk—like the one above, plus a few extra details. At that time I did not know who he was, nor that, in all probability, he was identical with the man who killed young Heilesen. (As a matter of fact he was acquitted because of insufficient evidence as regards this point after the Liberation.) I added that it was imperative that the man be rendered harmless, although I knew that this was more or less a death sentence. With the same object in view I repeated the description of him to the Danish police ten days later in Malmoe. A number of resistance people convened and sentenced the informer to death, but they did not manage to get within gunshot of him before he asked for sanctuary in the asylum set up for Danish informers in the Froslev camp. I feel convinced that if I had been informed that the man had been killed on my instigation it would only have given me a feeling of satisfaction. Likewise, I think that I should not have shrunk from shooting him myself if I had had the opportunity, provided of course that I had acquired the slightest idea of how to use a gun, and the necessary courage to enter into a duel with him.

What had happened to me in the course of those days in October? Was it this: had an ordinary man, a peace-loving, humane, rational human being, developed into a "killer"? And had the experience completely changed his character? Or was it the feeling which had oppressed me ever since the night in the loft in Humlebæk, which now—unnoticed by myself but unavoidably and inevitably—directed my view of our work until I admitted that anyone who in a state of war assumes the responsibility of life and death must also accept the conditions of war fully and consistently? The question was one of the most discussed problems with us—in all its generality—in the first impassioned postwar years. And, in my opinion also one of the most futile ones, because in the heat of the argument nobody realized that each person must base

175

his arguments on entirely different situations and experiences.

After the Liberation I met Paul Hennig in person, for the first and only time. It was in the police station. The police had asked me to have a talk with him to determine whether he was the informer from Humlebæk, a fact he had denied during the interrogations. He was exactly as Sig had described him, and it was not difficult to convince him that he had contributed to the breakdown of our group, which was, in any case, an inessential detail on his terrible list of sins during the persecution of the Jews. His appearance was quite ordinary, a rather good-looking man, the father of a little girl. His mother was German, he had gone to a German school, became a red-hot Nazi, and as such was fanatically convinced that the Jews were the source of all evil in the world. During the Occupation I wished that he could be wiped out as a noxious animal. Now it made quite an impression on me when the criminal inspector told me that undoubtedly he would be sentenced to death. And I felt it as a personal relief when in the Supreme Court, by a narrow majority of voices, he was let off with prison for life. After all he is a human being, and one should not kill a human being. Several have told me that they cannot see anything logical about it!

I soon agreed with Sig that we had fulfilled our obligations after this, and could make our preparations to leave the stage. First of all, we had to get Sig

176

out of the country. I took him down to my friend Mr. Borup Jensen, the teacher, where he would be more safe than in No. 33A, and from there I went to fetch his parents. Sig was the first of our group who had to escape. Both he and his family were very sorry about it. He had just started in business as an independent wholesale merchant, and he now had to see the basis of his whole future, which he had built up with so much trouble, in jeopardy. And nobody knew at that time that his good-by to his father when he stepped into the car would be the last. Mr. Sigtryggsson died at Christmas 1944 and never saw his only son again. I am glad that the last words I said to him, as he went back to the school from Borup Jensen's, were: "How happy and proud you must be to have such a son." I feel that those words pleased him very much. They were the last words that I, too, had the opportunity to say to my old headmaster before I had to leave the country.

Those who followed Bjarne Sigtryggsson's activity in Humlebæk, whether his colleagues or the Jews, will never forget him. It was a task which demanded the utmost. The fact that all there became interested and started collaborating with the helpers from Lyngby at once and that the transports were organized so quickly, is no doubt due more to Sig than to anybody else. He was young and like the rest of us he knew nothing about that kind of work. He felt impelled to help the persecuted, felt an urgent desire coupled with courage, practical sense, persistence, and, considering his age, an unusual authority. In the transport work there were people with a greater knowledge of the world and more maturity, but Sig was able to place all his time and strength at our disposal. I have never heard anybody who saw him work express any doubt that we picked the right man as the local leader. He became seriously ill up there with a rheumatic disease contracted after a laryngitis from the cold nights. Dr. Strandbygaard requested me urgently to see to it that he was sent home and put in a hospital. It was definitely a question of his life. The doctor thought that it was a kind of rheumatic fever. One of his legs was almost twice the size of the other, and he had great difficulty in walking and was in great pain. Sometimes he had to let somebody carry him. His illness, together with the immense responsibility, of which he was fully aware, must have been an almost superhuman burden for the young man, but he always refused to be careful, let alone withdraw. I know that he will protest against a valuation of his contribution in Humlebæk which emphasizes his work. And he is right that others too should be mentioned when I start evaluating individuals. But the entire spirit and attitude, which was the essential of the Lyngby Group and its work, is particularly beautifully characterized, I think, by the personality of my young colleague and his work during those exciting days.

The day after Sig had left for Sweden, Wienberg,

one of our helpers from Humlebæk, came to see me in Lyngby. He had been present at the dramatic episode near the Gylfe, but had been lucky enough to avoid both Gestapo guns and prison. Villumsen and three or four others from Humlebæk were already behind the bars at Vestre, the Copenhagen prison.

Wienberg told me that at the moment there were Danish and German Gestapo men walking all over Humlebæk asking for a certain Mr. Bertelsen. As far as I remember it was also on that occasion that, with some feeling of excited pride, I learned that there was a reward of 10,000 kroner for my apprehension. How the Germans paid the money to a fishmonger in Humlebæk, who escaped across the Sound with it and cheated the Germans with false information, is a detective story of its own (including disguise, false beard, secret eavesdropping) the mystery of which I have not been able to penetrate. One thing is certain, and that is that after we had heard Wienberg's story my wife and I felt impelled to make our preparations to do a vanishing trick from Lyngby. First of all I went to see Professor and Mrs. Ege. I told them what I had heard, and we discussed the matter at a meeting with Professor Ege's assistants, Mr. Linderstrom-Bang and Brandt Rehberg, and we soon agreed that for the time being I ought to become invisible—together with my family.

The same afternoon we put our house in order. I delegated the leadership of the group to Weeke, and

179

then went underground with my wife and children at some relatives at Holtug vicarage on Stevns. A week later, on my forty-second birthday as a matter of fact, Weeke visited us in the vicarage. He had talked to the police and they thought that the danger had blown over so much that my wife could return with the children. But he advised me to stay put for a couple of days more. I said good-by to my wife and children with an easy conscience. How was I to know that ten months were to lapse before I could meet my wife again in Sweden, and almost twenty until we could rejoin our children in Denmark after the Liberation.

In this respect we shared the fate of several others from the group. It was not long before we saw so many of them over there that, as a matter of fact, we could have continued the work of the Lyngby Group in the opposite direction: Sig, Nyskov, Larking, Villumsen (after a couple of months in the Vestre Prison and the Horserod prison camp), Wienberg, Miss Ulff, Skov Nielsen, Niels Andersen and his wife, Dr. Strandbygaard and Miss Christiansen, Mr. Lassen from Smidstrup, Hansen, the police sergeant from the gasoline office who had supplied us with coupons so we could get gasoline for our cars, and—last but not least—the Mexican from Humlebæk, to whose brilliant fortunes the group had contributed so generously. I closely watched the Mexican's development through all its stages on his way to sublimity—and fall, both during and after the Occupation. I do not

180

really recall any more whether—when like a shooting star he honored Sweden and my humble abode in Lund with his presence during the involuntary pause in his work for Denmark's liberation and his own enrichment—he introduced himself as skipper, captain, or contractor, or whether he had already reached the climax of his career and become a shipowner.

X

How Weeke Fooled the Gestapo

ᴓ

ON NOVEMBER 6 my wife and our children returned from our underground hiding place to our home in Lyngby. On the morning of November 9 she was arrested by the Gestapo. During an eight-hour cross-examination in Dagmarhus she refused to give the Germans the information they wanted, and she was sent to the Vestre Prison. She was told that she was being kept as a hostage and would not be set free until her husband had been caught. The same information was passed on to the Danish authorities and several of our friends, who applied to the German police. These were the conditions under which B. O. Weeke carried out an act under the nose of the Gestapo which attracted a lot of attention in resistance circles. The book by Dr. Gersfelt, which I have already mentioned, describes it briefly, and so does my wife in her narrative of her imprisonment. However, she tells the story only as far as she herself saw it in the prison. I think that a more detailed account of the circumstances, some of them naturally out of her ken, is necessary for the full comprehension of my wife's statement. It may also be of some interest as a small, yet despite everything cheerful contribution to the judgment of the relationship between Danes and Germans in those days.

On November 12, armed with a letter of introduction from the Danish Chief Director of the police and Deputy Police Commissioner Wolf, Weeke went up to Dagmarhus and asked to see my wife. When this was refused in gruff terms, and on the whole all negotiation was rejected as long as my wife refused to make a statement, this typically calm Dane got so stark, staring mad that he banged his fist on the table and raved in both Danish and German at the Germans' attitude. Arguments of such force could not but impress the men in the Gestapo's Danish auxiliary. Evidently they began to waver about their refusal, and after a brief discussion with the Gestapo, who had arrested and questioned my wife, permission was granted. On three conditions, however, which were not to be deviated from: First, Criminal Inspector Renner should be present all through the meeting. Second, they should speak in German. Third, Mrs. Bertelsen was not to be informed that her small daughter had not been arrested—as had been threatened.

Immediately, on their way down to Solje's car,

Weeke began his wooing of the Gestapo, and the soft words continued all the way to the prison. It was positively absurd that the Germans and the Danes could not agree. We ought to be the best friends in the whole world. Weeke knew many Germans thoroughly from numerous business trips. He had a great number of friends in Germany, and he was a close personal friend of Field Marshal Milcke, Göring's second in command (as a matter of fact, he had once met his sister): an outstanding and great man. What excellent people!

It is very unlikely that Renner managed to say one word during the short drive, and that was not the idea either, but Weeke's flow of words must have sounded like sweet music to his ears, which were not used to that kind of tone from the Danes. His mind was now tuned the way Weeke wanted it when they reached the place for his talk with my wife. How, during the questioning, he kept pulling the leg of the more and more confused Gestapo chief so that in the end he himself broke with all the three conditions laid down is told in my wife's narrative.

A minor, dramatic sequel to the questioning in the prison is Weeke's confrontation with Villumsen from the Gylfe. As Weeke and Renner were walking down the corridor of the prison Villumsen was led out of a questioning room and down the corridor in front of them, and suddenly when they walked right up behind him the German turned him round so that he faced Weeke.

"Do you know this man?" shouted Renner as he saw how startled Weeke was.

For a moment Weeke did not know what to do or say, for what had Villumsen said, and what did the Gestapo know? He elected to shake hands with him cordially. "I say, hello, Villumsen. Are you here?"

"So you do know him. From where?" The friendly tone had completely disappeared and the usual tone of the Gestapo had been substituted.

Weeke shielded his mouth with his hand and whispered confidently, "I'll tell you when we get down in the car."

When Solje had started the car the questioning continued. "Where do you know Villumsen from?"

"From Hotel Gylfe at Humlebæk."

"What were you doing there?"

"I took a parcel up there."

"From whom?"

"From Mrs. Bertelsen."

"What was in that parcel?"

"Money, I think."

"How much?"

"I would not know. But it was a big one. The size of a packet of sandwiches."

"But then you are involved too. You ought to be arrested!"

"I guess you are right, but we haven't time right now. First we must have some lunch!"

And then Weeke brought Renner down to Krogh's fish restaurant and ordered a lunch, which I think that few can do as well as Weeke. But it took a lot of schnapps before the cheerful atmosphere returned. During the conversation, when Renner enthusiastically exclaimed that what had impressed him most deeply as manifestations of Danish culture were the Danish schnapps and the Danish salami sausage, Weeke managed to persuade the owner to let him have a bottle of Aalborg Aqua-Vitæ and a salami sausage, which he presented to the Gestapo man, who by then had been reconciled completely. Mutual understanding shone all about when they parted!

The lunch at Krogh's became the preface to much "co-operation" between Weeke and the Gestapo in the service of a good cause. After another visit to my wife in the prison in order to get "information" about my probable whereabouts, Weeke started out on his raid of Jutland to fulfill a promise to the Gestapo about finding the vanished lecturer "dead or alive," if he was still in the country. The investigations finished at one of my friends, Dr. Bindslev's, in Skive. There as well as everywhere else the Resistance Movement was asked about Weeke, and all over Jutland it was confirmed that he worked for the Gestapo. The whole comedy was quite undangerous for any of the parties, but Weeke attained what he wanted: to "prove" that the rumor that Mr. Bertelsen "had gone across" should be interpreted as: across to Sweden, and not to Jutland, which was the second possibility. This in connection with incessant personal and more official applications for her release, which annoyed the Germans immensely—"We have almost half of Copenhagen coming here because of Mrs. Bertelsen," lamented Renner—brought about my wife's return home after nine days in prison.

There was a lot at stake for Weeke those days. At a party for the Ege and Lyngby groups after my wife's acquittal the poet of the party wrote: *Weeke's playing poker with the Gestapo, should not be tried da capo.* As a matter of fact Weeke did play his poker da capo, but in another way, with much at stake, and with good winnings, when he himself was sent to the Vestre Prison some time later. But that is a different story.

The real explanation why the first Danish hostage was set free will probably never be given. But I think that part of the truth is expressed in the following short abstract from a typical poetic product of the Occupation—written for the same occasion as the above. Connoisseurs will perceive the distinctive pathos of the same poetic genius, a world-famous professor and scientist: *Renner was so pleased with the spree, that little Mrs. Bertelsen he set free.*

These hints as a background for the understanding of my wife's narrative must necessarily be supplemented by a few details about the person who was the original cause of the small drama. The very morning my wife was arrested Weeke phoned me. He told me what had happened and asked me to leave Stevns immediately, as he expected that there might be a search for me out there the same afternoon. Here I must quote and correct Gersfelt's book, "The other members of the Lyngby Group were almost compelled to use force to prevent the schoolteacher from giving himself up to the Gestapo. By and by they managed to convince him that it would be nothing short of playing into the Germans' hand, and that the best thing he could do was to go to Sweden." In my opinion that is not true. Since the arrest of my wife I had not been in contact with the group in Lyngby, and at no time did I seriously intend to give myself up to the Gestapo. Primarily this was because I felt convinced that even if the Germans got hold of me they would not let my wife go free, and that, on the contrary, they would prefer to play us off against one another by questioning us separately. Secondly, I could not do it for the very reason that my arrest might mean disaster to a great number of people. I knew that the Germans considered it vitally important to catch me, since they had promised such a large reward for my arrest. Further, I had not forgotten what I had heard about the Gestapo cross-examination methods, and I had to consider it more than likely that if necessary they would apply these methods to me, though I could not possibly imagine that they would use them against my wife.

On November 16 I left my hiding place near Ringsted with some friends and went via Gjorslev to Sweden at the urgent request of my mother-in-law, who now lived with our children, and the Danish police authorities. It is rather a difficult matter to leave one's country under those circumstances, but I was in a way beyond everything. There was no alternative left when those who could best judge the situation emphasized that my wife's only chance was to make the Germans realize that it was not possible to get hold of me by retaining her. It was not necessary to "use force" against me, at least by anybody but myself, to make me decide. I wrote two letters about my escape, both of them intended for the Germans at Dagmarhus, but neither of them reached the addressee. One of them was directed to Mr. Højbjerg Christensen, Inspector of Education, and was written a few minutes before my departure, the other one was for my mother-in-law and went back on the boat that took me to Sweden.

I fled voluntarily, but in a mood that can hardly be understood by anybody else. That is probably the reason why the B.B.C., the illegal papers in Denmark, and the Swedish press all stated that I had reported at Dagmarhus asking the Germans to set free my wife instead.

Today it is in almost every respect unimportant.

189

but I still find it necessary to set down this correction as my final contribution to the story of the activities of the Lyngby Group. To any future historical analysis of this chapter of the Occupation, covering the German persecution of the Jews in Denmark, it may prove of some importance that what is written even in minor details should be as close in conformity with reality as possible.

XI

Sequel

BY GERDA BERTELSEN

NOVEMBER 9, 1943, was a Tuesday. In the morning when we woke up a thick, gray fog covered the roofs of the semidetached houses and the small gardens of Buddinge Lane. It was barely possible to discern that there were houses on the other side of the street, and it was completely impossible to perceive that behind the tall birches at the far end of the garden there was an open field with a path winding across it and up to the church.

The children had to get up and go to school, and for some reason or other we were a bit earlier than usual. I had almost finished dressing by a quarter past seven. Then the telephone rang, and a voice I did not recognize said that there was a "prairie schooner"—a canvas-covered truck—halfway down the street and German soldiers walking round looking at the numbers of the houses. They were carrying

191

guns. Nothing more was said. I hung up and rushed up the stairs. What could I do?

Somebody rang the doorbell violently. I tiptoed downstairs again, lifted the receiver off the telephone which was situated in the hall, and with nervous glances at the dark silhouettes behind the oblong, frosted window of the door, I dialed the police station in Lyngby, and then sneaked into the sitting room with the receiver in my hand, and closed the door firmly on the wire. I told the officer of the watch that I had just been informed that the Gestapo was coming, and could I get some help—quickly? They promised to be there right away.

I reckoned on five minutes' respite, and when the ringing was repeated, in order to draw out the time as long as possible I ran upstairs again into the room facing the street, opened the window and looked down. Outside the front door I saw a plain-clothes man. I asked, "Who is there?"

He looked up, and almost without any German accent he answered, "It's the police. You must open up."

I now realized that we were in serious trouble, and began feverishly to think of a way out. At least he would have to wait until I was fully dressed.

Outside, in the garden as well as in the street, there was nothing but fog. I ran down the stairs again, out through the back door and up to the back fence, over which I could see into our neighbors' house. They were having breakfast. I called, and Hansen came out. Breathless and by then more and more afraid, I told them what was going to happen, but as soon as he had said a few sympathetic words my worry for the children forced me back into the house. The ringing continued, and now something hard was knocked against the window in the door, and someone shouted angrily, "Open up!"

Finally I opened the door, and at once there was the plain-clothes man plus two soldiers with bayonets in the hall. I had only time to ask for his certificate of identity, and he was still holding his metal badge marked *Secret Police* in his hand, when three Danish policemen rushed in—was I glad to see them! But they did not look very happy, and of course they could not do anything. All the same, it did me a lot of good to see their kind faces, and to know that I did not face this ordeal alone.

The plain-clothes man scolded me and asked why I had called for the police. I told him that his foreign accent had convinced me that if he was a policeman, as he had said, he could not be a Danish policeman, and how was I to know he was not from the Hipos. He laughed contemptuously at that, and said that they did not eat anybody. *"Sie fressen keine Leute,"* he said, then: "Where is your husband?"

When I said that my husband was not at home, he ordered one of the Danish policemen to help him search the house. This was quickly done—they did

193

not even look into the attic. I had to accompany them. When I ventured a surprised remark and asked him why he had brought so many armed people, he said, "If your husband was desperate he might make a stand and start shooting."

I could not help laughing, "Don't worry, my husband would not even know how to handle a gun—if he ever saw one!"

He got very irritated at that and took it out on one of the Danish policemen. He threatened the Danish police and the entire Danish people. And then he turned to me.

"If we can't get your husband, we shall have to take you along for questioning, and keep you until your husband shows up. Put on some warm clothes, it's cold."

He did not answer my question whether I should bring my nightgown and toilet requisites. I told him I would not mind knowing whether I was coming back the same day, or if I was to be treated by the "Norwegian Methods," that is, if I was going to be made a hostage.

The children, who had dressed by now, came down the stairs and pressed themselves, terrified, against the wall and looked at us with big frightened eyes:

"Are you going to prison, Mom?"

The Gestapo looked at the children and said, "No, not to prison, only for questioning."

As if the poor kids knew the difference!

194

"Have you a maid or somebody who can take care of the children?" he asked.

"Yes, if you'll let me make a phone call."

He gestured toward the telephone, and remained by my side while I phoned the Borup Jensens. They were the first to enter my mind because, for one thing, it would not endanger our organization or themselves if their names were mentioned (as a matter of fact they were not; strangely enough it did not seem to interest the Gestapo a bit). Also, I had seen them the previous Sunday at Mr. Dige's, the Permanent Undersecretary, where we had discussed the present state of affairs.

I asked Grethe Borup Jensen to take care of the children. "The Germans are here to fetch me, Grethe," I told her.

Despite the shock she grasped the situation immediately, and having promised to pick up the children in a few minutes, she said, "Do you want me to phone the place where we met last Sunday?"

I thanked her, knowing that now my case would be referred to a quarter where it would be defended in every possible way by the best will and powers of our friends.

There was nothing more I could do—I had to go. I made the parting scene with the children as brief as possible, pretending that everything was all right and that they would soon have me back again. Tears came into their eyes and I had to be quick. On the front

195

steps I caught a glimpse of Mrs. Hansen coming through the fence into our garden.

"The children, let me have the kids," she called.

Then the subdued, sad figures disappeared in the gray morning fog, and the prairie schooner with its crossbar bottom and wooden seats along the sides came uncomfortably close and cut in front of me, and five or six Germans with their green uniforms and clanking guns awaited me.

Where were we going? That was my only thought as I sat there trying to seem outwardly cool and crunching an apple I had snatched from the bowl on the dining-room table. I dropped the core on the floor and lit a cigarette, all with a jaunty gesture—if only my hand had not shaken—well, it might have been because of the jolting of the truck. Where were we going? To the main street, then left, that's north-wards—Horserod Camp! I did not like that very much.

The fog had lifted a bit. Sorgenfri Palace! But now we turned left— Ah, then I knew whom they intended to catch besides me. I felt warm inside with delight as I knew that Prohaska was not at home! It was difficult to hide a triumphant smile as they rang his bell and knocked in vain. The great thing was to look as uninterested and innocent as possible—and that expression, I realized, ought preferably to stay on my face all the time. The truck turned round, we were going back to town and would finish the trip in the

196

prairie schooner at Dagmarhus, one of the Gestapo's two headquarters in Copenhagen.

This notorious building had many rooms. By now I have forgotten the numbers both of the questioning room and the cell in the Vestre Prison's German Ward for Women where I was confined. But for a long time afterwards I remembered these details whenever I met my fellow conspirators for a do-you-remember party.

The room we entered was an office with several tables and typewriters, large windows, and doors leading to other rooms. I was ordered to sit down in an armchair. There were a couple of them, and apparently they were intended for people who were waiting —and being watched. I sat there from eight until ten in the morning without anybody saying a word to me. Germans in uniform and plain clothes, Gestapo men I suppose, came and went. First my Gestapo man had a conference in an adjoining room, then he returned and talked to a man at a typewriter. In the course of the conversation I learned that his name was Renner, and that the man in the next room was called Hennig, the man at the typewriter Nagel.

As the door to Hennig's office was left ajar behind Renner I saw a bookcase with a long row of big files with the title: *Judenaktion in Denmark*. I also heard in passing the name of Larking, and then I knew that, despite their apparent forgetfulness as regards my person, the gentlemen were still discussing my case and our organization. Next Renner stopped near me and told another of the staff about a young man who the day before had been brought to Dagmarhus and had spent a couple of hours there waiting in the same room. It was obvious that he wanted me to hear the story, so he talked about the young man's nervousness and about his total breakdown when finally they had asked him why he sat there trembling and chattering. Well, he was waiting for the torture—and then the two chaps laughed and shrugged their shoulders at the idea that here at Dagmarhus anyone should dream of employing torture because somebody had distributed seditious papers! They only wanted to make me scared, and to put my nerves to a test, I felt.

I got stiff and tired of sitting down and got up to walk a few steps up and down, and I also walked toward the window, primarily to look out of the window, and secondly to have a look at a painting between the two windows representing a man in a uniform.

"Sit down!" said an irritated voice.

"Who is that man?" I said pointing at the painting.

"Field Marshal Rommel," answered Nagel briefly.

Next Renner returned from Hennig's office and asked if I cared for a cup of coffee in the canteen. I said yes, please, for who could tell when I might get out of there, and I needed a pick-me-up.

I had never before been accompanied by such satellites as Nagel and Renner, and I shuddered when we got out into the street and walked the few paces to the canteen. How badly I felt! The word "interrogation" was in my mind all the time. When was it coming? Would I be able to handle it and calmly tell them the invented story—for their pleasure—including the few unimportant names which my husband and I had agreed on while we were at Stevns? I had never thought for a minute that I should really need them. And where was the red herring through it all? Could I remember and stick to it? Villumsen arrested, Sig in Sweden, place names like Gylfe and Humlebæk, my husband gone, I did not know where. All those things were unquestionably true.

Coffee was served, and rolls. They helped a bit. But then Renner said pointedly, "Now tell us, where is your husband?"

"I don't know," I said, "and furthermore, I will not be questioned by you in a restaurant. I expect to be taken to your superiors, and demand that everything be handled properly."

The two men looked at each other, and with his face red with anger Renner said: "We are quite used to the impudent behavior of you Danes. If you don't like to sit at the same table with us, you are welcome to move and find one for yourself. We don't mind. Moreover," he continued a little more gently, "I hate to listen to the lies of a woman who, judging by her position and appearance, should be of high moral quality. I would rather that you said that you refuse to tell us where your husband is. That sounds better."

"All right," I said, offended, "have it your own way. I am not going to tell you!" The meal was finished in uncomfortable silence. Then the gentlemen got up, so I had to get up, too, and go back to my waiting.

There I sat again, looking at Rommel and listening to the voices as before. What would be the next move? And when would I be questioned? Had a message been sent to Stevns to warn my husband, and what would he do? I hoped that he would go to Sweden as soon as possible. If the Gestapo got hold of him they would play us off against each other, and there would be no end of trouble for all of us. And who could believe in their promise that I would be set free, if my husband gave himself up? No man in his senses would.

Renner entered, in overcoat and with a brief case. He stuffed a towel into it, and announced that he was going down to the public baths.

Then it was Nagel's turn to take care of me. Renner had talked to me in Danish all the time, but Nagel could not speak a word of Danish. Now it was really a question of being on the alert. Should I ask for an interpreter? As a matter of fact, Nagel looked quite nice and kind, and he had a picture of two children standing on his table. When he saw that I was looking at it, he handed it to me, explaining that his wife and children lived in Hamburg.

The paper stuck in the typewriter. Nagel adjusted it, and then suddenly turned to me.

"Sit down beside me. I am going to make a report. Let us start with your husband's name in full, position, birthday and year. Political views? Your own data?" He took it down with nods and shrugs of his shoulder, and was surprised when I said that I was not a member of any woman's organizations. Then he looked in surprise at my husband's birth date.

"You are not telling me that you don't know where your husband was on his birthday. I suppose you were with him, weren't you? You must have been. Where were you on November 6?"

I looked at my watch. It was two in the afternoon. The danger ought to be over by now, and a message should have reached Stevns so my husband could get away in safety. No, I dared not, after all. In that moment the door to Hennig's office was opened, and he came out smiling affably—the man who had ruined our Humlebæk route, sent Villumsen to prison, and hunted Sig across the ploughed fields, bullets whizzing past him. I recognized him from the description the elder Sigtryggsson had given us. I could not be mistaken. He had been in the headmaster's house and threatened Sig's parents. They had had time to fix his features in their minds.

I felt myself turning pale, and the sweat of fear

chilled my temples and spine so that I shuddered.
What now?

He offered me cigarettes, and a cookie from a tin.
I refused the cookies but accepted a cigarette, and
regretted it at once when I saw how both of them
stared at my hand holding the cigarette while Hennig
lit it with his lighter. However, the relief that for a
moment attention had been directed from my husband
and his doings supported me, and when now, with
emphasis, Nagel pointed out, "We know that you have
participated in helping Jews to Sweden, isn't that
true?" I answered calmly: "Of course it is, all decent
people did."

I think that that was exactly what Hennig had been
waiting for. For now followed a lecture, spoken in a
soft tone and with a torrent of volubility, on the misfortune and abasement it was for an Aryan to get
involved with a Jew. He used the "Jew Baby" term,
attempting to arouse my disdain.

"There are Jews in this country," he continued,
"whom we can render harmless by merely removing
their money. That is not the kind of Jew we want to
get at. It is the goddamn Jew from the east, who runs
around on his flat feet, whom we must destroy!"

Yes, he knew his lesson. For a moment I allowed
my thoughts to travel back to the desperate scenes
that took place when the Jews were shipped off to
Theresienstadt, and where part Jews or Jews married
to Aryans had complained because they were treated

just like those of completely Jewish blood. It could not be denied, here was quite a new dividing line, described by Hennig, which still more poignantly underlined the casual and cruel game, with human lives at stake, which was being played in those days—in *our* days. Did these dividing lines exist at all? Weren't they human beings all of them?

"And why did you help the Jews? Was it to make money?" interrupted Nagel looking at my clothes; however, he did not find them excessively elegant, obviously.

"Because of sympathy with poor, persecuted people, who came to us confidently placing their lives and fates in our hands," I answered.

There was Hennig again: "Don't you know that Germany is the only state in the world which has solved the racial problem in a humane way? What has the United States done? They have land enough, but have they given any land to the Jews or the colored people? No, but Germany has allowed the Jews to decide for themselves in Theresienstadt."

What else could I answer but that I thought that it was more humane to let people live where they wanted to live.

"You mentioned sympathy a little while ago," said Nagel, "but do you ever think of the poor women and children in Hamburg, who are the victims of the Anglo-Jewish bombs?"

No, now I had to tune down my spirit of opposition.

This was nothing short of wrangling, and where would I be tomorrow if I continued as I had started? I shut my mouth, and from then on opened it only to answer questions of who, where, and how, as my husband and I had agreed.

In the end the report was finished, lacking only the information about my husband's whereabouts.

At that time Renner returned, refreshed and fit, and he started right away reading the report. But after a superficial perusal he threw it back to Nagel, banged his fist on the table, and shouted, "You know more than that! You know more names. Prohaska, for instance."

I shook my head.

"Your husband then, he must know somebody at the Technical High School?"

"It's very likely," I answered. "My husband knows a lot more people than I do."

"We are going to take your daughter, she was probably present at her father's birthday together with you. She is eleven years old, so she must be able to give us some information, but it is your own fault if she gets a nervous breakdown."

That was carrying it too far! I looked at Renner, who was pacing up and down the room, and at Nagel, who was sitting motionless at his typewriter. I was tired, it was late in the afternoon, and the threat about taking my daughter worried me.

Then I remembered an incident I had heard about

204

not long ago. There might be some kind of consolation in that. A doctor of our acquaintance had been arrested and questioned, suspected of having been an intermediary at a dispatch of some illegal kind. He was asked whether he was married or engaged, and whether his mother was alive. Then they would send for her. He then confessed, but had regretted it since, for on second thought he did not believe that they would have carried out their threat. But while he was being questioned, and was oppressed by the situation and panic-stricken at the thought that his old, weak mother might have to pay for his doings, he began to waver.

So I looked Renner straight into the eyes and said, "You do not even know where she is."

"I'll find out!" he shouted furiously. "I'll ask the Danish police. They won't dare to deny me any information!" Then he rushed out of the room and banged the door behind him. I did not see him till four days later.

Hennig had withdrawn in the meantime, but Nagel had more on his mind.

"We have heard rumors to the effect that your husband has run off with 4,000 kroner, and that he has been seen in restaurants in company with ladies."

Despite all my worries, I could not help smiling. If they were interested in such trifles, there was hope left that they did not know anything about the Lyngby Group and its activities.

"If my husband wanted to enrich himself," I answered, "he could have taken bigger amounts. Four thousand kroner isn't much nowadays."

"And what was your role in the operation?" asked Nagel.

"Oh, I looked after the house and the telephone. I never went to Humlebæk, and I don't know what my husband was doing there."

I think that by then Nagel, too, was a bit tired. The subject of ladies and restaurants was not bad, though. We could have talked a lot about that. It must have been rumored that we were regular visitors at the Bellevue, where for some time we had a marvelous sanctuary when things got too hot in the house with the blue curtains in Buddinge Lane, but evidently Nagel had not got enough to build on, and instead he returned to his original theme.

"Isn't it true that there's a coldness between you and your husband? One might think so, since you were not together on his birthday. Let's get this over with. Where were you?" His voice grew stricter, and he eyed me fixedly, "You are an intelligent woman—if you don't tell me the truth now you will end up in the Vestre Prison among the riffraff. You'll be ashamed to be seen in their company. Your children, too, will be ashamed of you when they grow up and understand what their mother did."

It was almost four in the afternoon. It was very tempting, since my husband no doubt was in safety somewhere in southern Zealand, to tell him about our place of refuge in the vicarage in Holtug. Then I could get back home today. But, no—who had promised me that? I shook my head. All right, I felt, I'd go to jail if I must, and be satisfied if that was all that happened to me.

A sergeant major was sent for, and I was ordered downstairs and into a car which took me to the Vestre Prison. A strange drive through well-known streets, seeing well-known faces among the passersby—so near at hand that I gasped, suppressing a cry. A little later the large, forbidding building towered up in front of the car and swallowed me, as it had swallowed so many others.

In the arrival room I was measured and weighed, and put into a stall just like a piece of lost property left to be picked up later. But when, and by whom?

It was embarrassing having to undress and be searched by a strange woman. Even more embarrassing—she was a Dane. And terrible to see the door closing behind one, and to hear the key being turned in the lock. And what despair to be alone with one's confused thoughts. Nine paces one way, nine paces the other, up and down the tiled floor of the cell. The hard plank bed, the barred window so high up, the nasty washbasin in the corner—that was the sort of interior multitudes of Danish citizens learned to know during the Occupation.

207

The food was edible, but was not eaten, for the very simple reason that I was not hungry. I was too busy turning over in my mind all that had been said at the questioning, and wondering what might happen next time. Then came the incessant, gnawing thought of the children. And what had actually happened to my husband? Even if he had managed to get away in the first instance there were still many possibilities of getting caught before sunset. Would he succeed in getting across to Sweden? I hoped so constantly, but I knew nothing. That was the worst of it.

During the exercise period I caught glimpses of my fellow prisoners from the ward, but soldiers stood along the pathway and saw to it that we did not speak to each other. As far as I could see I did not know any of them. But what use if I had? I felt as if I was walking on boggy ground, because I was hiding a secret about a group of people whose lives might depend on whether I was able to act as if I did not know anything. For the time being it would only be harmful for anyone to get into contact with me. And if I were to be helped, the help would have to come from the outside. I had never felt so lonely and isolated before.

Wednesday passed and so did Thursday. A parcel containing clothes, cigarettes, butter, and chocolate showed me that somebody was thinking of me, but I did not know who it was. I could not sleep, only walk up and down, and turn over and over what I had said and done. Wednesday night was St. Martin's Eve, and there was an extra supper, two small pieces of smoked eel, which I sent back untouched, much to the surprise of the personnel. Their faces were almost worried when they came to collect the tray after each meal. When I complained of the cold a sergeant major was sent for. He returned with the Danish female warder to have a look at the radiator. I heard him ask her, "What kind of prisoner is she?" She murmured, "Something about the Jews." "Oh," he said, shrugged his shoulders and left. But I got a different cell.

A German female warder was rather more communicative and liked to tell me about the other prisoners. One day there was a row in the corridor and a lot of shouting in both German and Danish. Later on she told me that a girl who had given birth to child in the prison had refused to do anything whatsoever to take care of it, and went absolutely crazy when she was reproached because of the mess and disorder in her cell.

Every day an afternoon paper came, and books, too, and I could see that other prisoners had had them before me. There were scribbles and scratchings in them, but they made no sense, and I found no messages.

Friday the 12th brought a change. There was a message that I was to be questioned. Full of grave misgivings, I walked down the stairs and was met by Renner and Weeke. What had happened? Why was he here? If I had been nervous at the prospect before, I was now stiff with fear. Had Weeke been arrested? And the organization exposed? Was everything over?

Renner led us into a questioning room and ordered that we should be placed on either side of the table while he himself sat down at the end. He looked angry and sulky, and said, "This is an interrogation, not a social call. Visits are only for those who behave, and you won't talk."

So there we were. I supposed Renner ought to do the talking, but what was wrong with him? Weeke's presence made everything seem unusual and he appeared very nervous. Renner started by demanding that we should speak German, but Weeke had so much on his mind that he could hardly pronounce the words properly, and it did not take long before he reverted to Danish. "It'll be better this way," he said and winked at me, and then he really started in to talk. Nothing could stop the spate of words. He told me that the children were all right, that my mother had come to stay with them, and that I myself would be set free and be allowed to go home, if only I would tell them where my husband was, so we could get hold of him. I was speechless. Had I heard right? "It's better this way," Weeke repeated, "so go on: talk!"

A wee bit of light dawned on me, I cheered up and took heart. As soon as I mentioned Holtug vicarage Weeke jumped up and said to Renner, "Now I suggest that we phone the vicar and ask to talk to Mr. Bertelsen, we've got to get things started."

And the incredible thing happened: Renner went out to the telephone and left us alone! In that split second I got the explanation of all the things that baffled me. My husband was safe, and his chances of getting across to Sweden were excellent. We only had to pretend that we would help them to find him and make him return. I was a hostage in the Vestre Prison, and many influential people had been approached to get me out again. The only thing was not to lose patience for a little while longer. Weeke would try to come back in a couple of days.

Of course the result of the phone call was negative. Pastor Ellebjerg answered briefly and coldly that he did not know anything about Mr. Bertelsen's whereabouts. That was all we wanted to hear, and I quickly hung up.

We sat down at the table again, and looked at one another. What now? Renner probably thought that it was his turn to make a move, and launched into a protracted, severe lecture on the folly of participating in illegal relief actions. It was much too dangerous. I should realize that if they caught my husband during his attempted escape it would mean the concentration camps in Germany for him, and the Horserod Prison Camp for me. And they would leave me there until everybody had forgotten about me. Weeke inter-

211

rupted him, remarking that my husband was a teacher of divinity, and as such must have intervened for idealistic reasons! This gave Renner a chance to expatiate on Germany as a country of law and justice and the Germans as the true idealists.

"You Danes are a ridiculous people," he said; "you walk around with the royal insignia in your buttonhole, but were any of you willing to die for your King? We, however, are all willing to die for our Führer. The German people is a nation of heroes!"

When we had recovered somewhat from those outporings—answered in our own secret thoughts—he asked me another direct question.

"Do you know Villumsen, and where have you seen him?"

When I answered in the negative, he got furious again: we Jew-Helpers were only tiresome and stupid. There was a queue of fishermen every day at Dagmarhus reporting that they had been tricked out of so many thousand kroner, and there were even Jews who wanted information about relatives who had disappeared—and most stupid of all, there were people who were offering money to get me out of jail. As if money meant anything at all. "The Bertelsen case has already cost us 10,000 kroner. Has that money been spent on sending saboteurs to Sweden or on purchase of arms?"

We were getting into troubled waters again, and Weeke hastily interrupted:

"You understand, no doubt, Mr. Criminal Inspector, that a man who like Bertelsen is induced by religious feelings—well, he even wrote a book on the Old Testament—could not possibly be dragged into anything connected with saboteurs and arms. You must understand that. By the way," he hurried on, "there is a thing we haven't talked to Mrs. Bertelsen about. What was it now that I was not to mention?"

"That her small girl has not been questioned," answered Renner, who by then was completely entangled in Weeke's web of irrelevant talk. He looked at me meaningly, hoping for my appreciation.

"That's right," shouted Weeke, "and why not, Mrs. Bertelsen?"

I was not really in the mood to solve riddles, and by this time was completely dazed by Weeke's complicated tactics and dangerous attempts to coax the Gestapo man out of his inquisitive mood, so I answered acidly, "Oh, I suppose it wasn't any use."

"No!" And now Weeke jumped up from his chair and went up to Renner and beat him on the shoulder with a bang, grimacing and winking at me, "It's because there is a kind heart beating in the chest of this worthy man!" And sitting down again he took my hand and said impressively, "Now tell us why was it that Inger was not questioned, Mrs. Bertelsen?"

Then, finally, I understood what lay beneath these strange tactics, and with a feeling of embarrassment I

213

forced my lips to pronounce the words I knew Renner wanted to hear.

"He had not the heart to arrest a child." Renner beamed.

What I also understood was that Weeke was playing a very dangerous game, the outcome of which was dependent on his audacity and presence of mind while he was near the three Gestapo men. He was like a man strolling around in a lion's den, and I shuddered at the thought of what he was exposed to.

I startled when for the third time Renner reverted to Villumsen's name and suggested that he should be brought up from his cell to be confronted with us. Weeke managed to ward it off. He got up and said:

"Well, I have got to go and see if I can find Bertelsen, so Mrs. Bertelsen can get back to her children." That was the end of the questioning.

Then the days passed by slowly again, Saturday, Sunday, Monday. More uncertainty, more fear at the thought of our audacious enterprise. No sleep, no rest.

Weeke returned Tuesday, without Renner. A young German female warder, who used to see the prisoners to the washrooms and back, sat at the table with us. This time he told me that my husband had "got across all right," and what that meant nobody knew for the time being, said Weeke with a wink to me, which the woman did not see. But it might mean to Sweden; however, it was more probable that it meant to Jutland, where there were several places well suited for someone who wanted to hide himself. If now I would only tell him the names and addresses of people we knew and who I thought might help my husband, Weeke would spare no trouble to find the refugee's hide-out and bring him back.

Again I was stupefied, but did what I had been told in blind obedience and confidence that there must be some sense behind it all, and Weeke wrote it all down in his notebook. The more names and addresses I mentioned the more difficult it was for me to keep a straight face. It was all beginning to look like a farce.

But I was still a prisoner in the Vestre Prison, and the play still lacked a final act. We said good-by, and I went back to my cell.

Doubt and hope alternated again. But gradually I began to feel convinced that everything would turn out all right. Weeke's visit had poured optimism into my heart. By taking over the part of the pursuer he had managed to turn away the Gestapo's interest from my husband. Indeed, Renner himself had said that he would not waste time and men on the search. They had me and could take things easy. It was in my own interest to make my husband turn up.

Weeke's play acting also increased my husband's chances of finding a place from which to cross to Sweden in safety. And what use was I then to the Germans when they realized that my husband had gone and could not be brought into the open again?

I was set free on the 18th. Weeke and Nagel were waiting downstairs when I was "served out," having signed a declaration about abstaining, under penalty, from any anti-German activities in the future.

XII

Leaves from a Diary

BY AAGE BERTELSEN

Malmoe, November 23, 1943

TONIGHT AGAIN the evening news broadcast of the Swedish Broadcasting Corporation gives us the information we fear but can't do without. Sabotage in Denmark is making great progress, and so are the countermeasures: last night they executed two saboteurs, one because he was carrying a crowbar under his coat when he tried to buy a gun from a German soldier. The broadcast stated that he had not used the crowbar, but had intended to knock the German over the head if he did not hand over the gun without making trouble. I wonder how they got that confession out of him.

Aage Nielsen, who died while being tortured in prison, told his parents, who oddly enough were allowed to visit him shortly before he died, that he had but one wish left: for the Germans to shoot him. It was R. J., a mechanic and a saboteur, who'd told me about it just before I sent him across to Sweden via X. It was in his workshop that Aage Nielsen had made his bombs. R. J. was wanted and had the Gestapo close on his heels. No wonder that he struck me as very nervous. He knew what was waiting for him if he got caught.

Aage Nielsen's parents were not able to recognize their son. He had lost his left eye, his fingers were broken, and he had no nails, and moreover he was almost insane with thirst. It is a tried and true measure against an unmanageable prisoner, who will not give in, to fill his food with pepper and salt to induce thirst —however, in this case it did not work. The young baker with the crowbar was spared all this, at least in the end. He got what Aage Nielsen asked for in vain: a bullet.

The news tonight makes me remember another broadcasting incident. It was during one of the first days of the German occupation, April 12, 1940. I was sitting in the same room as now in the home of the same good friends, only that night I was alone in the house. Sven Svensson and his wife and their two small girls had gone away to some place or other in Southern Sweden like many other people from Malmoe whom the authorities had requested to leave town because of the imminent danger of war. After the news about the events in Denmark and Norway the Swedish Prime Minister Per Albin Hansson came on the air. His speech was one of the utmost gravity. It was possible, he thought—and we understood that he considered it very likely—that a foreign power had the same plans for Sweden as for the two other Scandinavian countries. It should be known, however, that in that case the Swedes would fight till the end with all means at their disposal. It was a very unreserved speech, one of the most vigorous speeches I have heard by a statesman.

Gradually it grew dark in the room, and we were not allowed to turn on the light. Malmoe was blacked out for the first time, and nobody had blackout curtains. I turned the radio on again. This time there was music from Stockholm: Beethoven's violin concerto played by Telmanyi and a symphony orchestra. I am sure that as long as I live I shall remember that broadcast. Beethoven interpreted by a maestro, an experience which was intensified into an impression for life by the consciousness that any minute we might hear German bombers overhead. Beethoven and Hitler! It is highly improbable that two more powerful expressions of the differences within German spiritual life could be imagined. At that time I still believed that Beethoven's spirit remained alive in the German people, and that in the long run it would be victorious. I also consoled myself, amid grief at my country's disaster, which took place during my stay as an "exchange lecturer" in our brother country, by the

219

knowledge that my people and nation had been spared actual war, and that my own family and house were safe.

Today sabotage is burning and crashing all over Denmark. My wife is in a German prison in Copenhagen. Six men from the Gestapo with police cars and tommy-guns took her away fourteen days ago in the presence of our children. They have tried to make her believe that they have arrested Inger, whose eleventh birthday we celebrated the last day we were together in our hiding place. But I doubt that it will make Gerda give them more information.

Tonight the radio also gives reports from the fronts, and what we hear is unambiguous and much more cheerful than what we hear from Denmark. Let them rage as much as they like. It is possible that Beethoven's spirit may or may not be dead in the German people, but Hitler's evil spirit is on the threshold of death anyway.

Epilogue

On Anti-Semitism

I HOPE that this book has succeeded in reproducing the most essential features of the work of the Lyngby Group and in picturing people and conditions as we saw them during the persecution. It has seemed most important to me that the basic atmosphere which helped us through those dark nights and days should again be crystallized in this report. We saw—as I find it—the kindness of the Danish heart, Danish enthusiasm, and the Danish sense of humor like a high bridge spanning an abyss of horror. In spite of everything the memory of those days is endowed with a gleam of high spirits, *hilaritas,* which according to Spinoza's psychology is the natural attitude of free men toward life. Yet there is also a drop to the sense of despair which according to Theodor Herzl, the founder of Neo-Zionism, is an element of every unusual enterprise in the service of a great cause.

And here I might well finish. However, it is not possible for me to set a full stop to this account without taking this opportunity to put forward some more

221

general and personal views. The knowledge of the Jews I acquired then, supported and enlarged by my daily personal contact with Jewish refugees through eighteen months spent in Sweden plus several years of study of the history and religion of the Jewish people probably give me some title and also an obligation to air my views in an epilogue on the history of anti-Semitism, which I met at close range. As a matter of fact, it has been my intention from the beginning that the book as a whole should be a contribution to the debate on the Jewish problem, and preferably—if modestly—a contribution to the struggle against anti-Semitism. To some degree it is a sort of continuation of the work of October 1943.

The persecution of Jews in Denmark was a single episode in Hitler's attempt to eradicate the Jews from the earth—an attempt that led five million people to death. Five million! That is five hundred times as many as the victims of the fatal night of St. Bartholomew, on which the casualties are estimated in history to have been about ten thousand. But it is hardly likely that it releases correspondingly strong feelings. Five million people in the gas-chambers are more than the whole population of Denmark. It is a figure which the mind may well grasp, but our hearts cannot comprehend. It is like certain astronomical distances which exceed the human imagination and consequently do not sink in deeply enough to leave a lasting impression. During their 1900 years

222

of exile the Jews have been persecuted, tortured, and killed, but the persecutions of our time in Germany and in the countries occupied by the Germans not only exceed any single former pogrom but also the persons affected in *all* previous persecutions. Add to this the devilish sadism which is evidenced in the reports on the persecutions. What happened here was, as Hugo Valentin had it, not only the biggest pogrom in the history of man, but it was also the biggest sadistic genocide of history.

In this darkness of barbarism and horror, the story of the persecutions in Denmark is a bright spot. Of the six to seven thousand Jews living in this country only 475 were caught and sent to concentration camps. The rest was successfully brought to Sweden. So far it has been an unsolved riddle why the Danish Jews, who were transported to Theresienstadt along with some thousands from other countries, did not share the fate of all the others. They were neither treated with cruelty nor killed. The historical explanation is probably given in my wife's report of her interrogation in the Dagmarhus.

The Gestapo's reference to the "fact" that Hitler was the only one who has been able to solve the Jewish problem in a humane way by gathering them together at Theresienstadt seems to indicate that the Bohemian concentration camp was intended as an excuse for the cruel, sadistic wholesale murderer, and a defense to be used in case of accusations from the rest of the world. It was, so to speak, a piece of propaganda of the same kind as the idea of Denmark as Hitler's "model protectorate" as compared with all the other oppressed countries. Probably the German people as a whole did not know what was happening in Maidanek and Auschwitz. Is it possible that even the Gestapo at Dagmarhus spoke in good faith when they exalted the German racial policy at the expense of the democratic countries? The question can hardly be answered now, but one would like to be able to believe that even among the Gestapo there were people who, although they wanted to contribute toward a "settlement" of the Jewish problem through concentration camps according to the classical and dictatorial model, were not interested in becoming purveyors to Hitler's gas-chambers.

Ever since the Jews have existed as the "chosen people" among the other peoples of the world without their own national center they have been continually threatened by persecution. It is to be hoped that by the foundation of the State of Israel on May 14, 1948, actual progroms will be precluded in the future. Not only as far as the Jews are concerned, but for the whole of the civilized world this event is one of the happiest in the history of mankind. In the name of humanity it must be wished sincerely that the new country will grow bigger and stronger until it can support the Jews in other countries and absorb all those who seek shelter within its frontiers, besides all those who of their own free will want to become citizens of the promised and restored land.

Yet even though actual persecutions involving death may cease in the future, the ghost of anti-Semitism has not yet been exorcised. Even the first president of Israel, the greatest name among the Jewish people today, the late Dr. Chaim Weizmann, has summed up—before an Anglo-American investigating committee—his view of postwar anti-Semitism in the following despondent announcement:

> "It hurts me deeply, but I do not see how we can stop it, or what can be done about it. Anti-Semitism is a sort of disease which is spreading apparently in accordance with its own laws. I only hope that it will never reach the terrible dimensions it reached in Europe. As a matter of fact I imagine for some reason or other that the Anglo-Saxon countries are immune from it. But it is a hope, a pious hope—and when I look at Canada, South Africa, even Great Britain, and even U.S.A., I sometimes lose my freedom from fear. I believe that the only fundamental reason for the anti-Semitism is—it may seem tautologic—that the Jews exist. We seem to carry anti-Semitism in our knapsacks wherever we go."

Weizmann's words express an old Jewish feeling; his skepticism does not fall short of the hopelessness we meet with in the Talmud parable: *If the pitcher fall on the stone the pitcher will break, if the stone fall on the pitcher the pitcher will break—so one way or another, poor pitcher.*

Arthur Koestler, who refers to Weizmann's statement in his book *Promise and Fulfilment: Palestine 1917-1949,* has a brighter outlook. He thinks that at the present moment, for the first time since Palestine's downfall at the beginning of the Christian era, there is a chance of putting an end to the Jewish problem. Whether it will be successful depends on the Jews themselves. The new Israel has created a new situation, says Koestler. To deny one's connection with the Jews before 1948 was tantamount to denying one's solidarity with the persecuted people and, consequently, an unpermissible, cowardly self-abandonment. In decency the Jews had to feel that they were bound by an old heritage which was not yet fulfilled. Today, however, every Jew is free to choose whether he wants to be a Jew among Jews in Israel, or to be assimilated by the people among whom he lives. Since the setting up of the Hebrew state, the Jew who refuses to go to Israel but who at the same time asks to retain a religious community separating him from his fellow citizens is in a sense guilty of an "untenable anachronism," Koestler says. Orthodox Judaism, which is tied up with certain national and perhaps racial conceptions, should be maintained only within Israel, he thinks. The others, those "in segregation," will have to take the consequence of the changed

226

conditions for the Jewish people and give up their religion in its traditional shape.

It is difficult to share Koestler's belief that the Jews themselves by making their choice between this *either-or* should be able to solve the problem of anti-Semitism. For one thing it appears rather improbable that orthodox believers, who live comfortably in countries where they are granted absolute religious liberty, would wish to go to Israel, for reasons which to them would seem to be abstract and purely philosophical. And for another thing, the Jewish problem is more than a religious one—today it is not even primarily religious. Their religion is a factor which intensifies the tension between the Jews and the people among whom they live, but it is far from the decisive one. How many of those people who air their definite views on the Jews have ever seen an orthodox Jew, or even had any personal impression of his religion? Today's anti-Semitism is undoubtedly to a far higher degree connected with what—to use a vague and untenable expression—is called race. It comes to the fore wherever to any great extent the Jews make themselves felt, and wherever they attract the attention of the majority because of their appearance, their manners, their doings, names, and economic status, and, if occasion should arise, their religion. A very revealing indication of the origin of the Jewish problem is found in the tragic, linguistic, and historical fact that our word for *guest* has the same root as the Latin word *hostis,* meaning enemy. This goes to show that antisemitism is really not unique. It is a special case within an ordinary psychological phenomenon, that of hatred for strangers, aversion for the minority who differ perceptibly from the prevailing standard within the national, public, racial, and religious community. It is the tragedy of the Jewish people that as a "people in segregation" in many parts of the world they have become the minority people par excellence.

Anti-Semitism is *the* minority problem of all minority problems and, consequently, is also a deep-rooted and world-wide cultural problem, more so as the civilization of the Western countries is built on the conviction of the sanctity of the individual and the right of the minority. Therefore it is absolutely necessary, in the name of civilization and humanity, to insist on the right of the Jews, even the orthodox Jews, to live their lives within the framework of a civic community in conformity with their traditions, their philosophy, and their religion. One of the supporting pillars of our democratic civilization is shaken when anti-Semitism gets the upper hand.

During their time the Nazis understood that and used it. In a letter of June 22, 1944, to the SS officials, Dr. Best, the representative of the German Reich in Denmark during the persecution of the Jews, said: *The Jewish problem is the dynamite we use to blow up the fortifications in which the last sharpshooter of*

228

liberalism has entrenched himself. The nations which give up their Jews thereby leave their former Judaized mode of life which was based on false ideals of freedom. Not until then can they take up their position in the struggle for a new world.

Best was right when he considered the persecution of Jews a decisive means to ruin Western civilization and its democratic ideals of freedom. It was not only the Jews who were threatened by destruction by the Nazis. It was our very civilization, the moment we surrendered our Jews to their pursuers.

It is always civilization which is at stake when anti-Semitism enters the picture. Under direct persecution there is no problem at all for decent people; however, in normal everyday times it may be difficult to fight against this many-headed monster, since it is true that anti-Semitism is vigorously allied with deep-rooted tendencies in our character. Anti-Semitism is a decisive cultural problem, but also a pressing psychological problem for every individual, for there is no denying that it is rooted in the very conception of civilization that we shall cultivate the human mind, trying to purge or check the bad instincts.

History, and especially the history of modern times, is full of instances which show that hate against the stranger may make itself felt in any mind with the strength of an instinct. Many know from experience that they have to be on the lookout for these dangerous tendencies within themselves.

229

I remember from the first day of my stay as a refugee in Sweden how, at my evening visit to the Danish club in Malmoe, I stopped on the threshold, startled, as I looked across the room. All of a sudden I here found myself in a crowd of some two hundred countrymen, Danes who nearly all of them had dark hair, dark eyes, and pale complexions. I noticed all right that I was among friends, but all the same I think that my very surprise in that moment proves the existence of the germ of a certain aversion, which under special conditions might develop into anti-Semitism of some kind. If that is true, I should like to add that as far as I know the germ was never allowed to germinate. But it was probably quite a usual experience among the Danish refugees in Sweden that the plentiful, and in the beginning numerically dominant, group of Danish Jews was the cause for friction which quite frequently caused difficulties.

On top of the involuntary dislike for aliens, when they constitute an important fraction within one's own territory, there is also a considerable reason for anti-Semitism in the inveterate human tendency to draw general conclusions and to pass general sentences based on isolated, individual cases. Everybody knows the traditional clichés about the Jews, and many consider them established facts without giving them a second thought. Jews are greedy and stingy, they are obtrusive, they are as thick as thieves, and so on and so forth. During my lifetime I have met several hundred people of Jewish descent, and for a long period I had the closest possible contact with them, both Danish Jews and foreign, but it is not possible for me to say anything in general about them for the very reason that they are individually just as different as are we. There are bad Jews and good ones among them just as among all other people, or rather they are a mixture of more or less valuable qualities—just like their non-Jewish countrymen. There are people who maintain that the Jews have certain dominating characteristics. I cannot allow myself to express any opinion on this. My experience with them has been too slight—or perhaps too great—to warrant my making a statement. "The Jew as such" is most definitely and most easily characterized by those who are not distracted by experiences and facts. As far as I am concerned, I know only the individual human being as a fellow man and a countryman. "The Jew" in general is a cliché I do not understand, just as it is impossible for me to pin a common label on a Copenhagen errand boy or a West Jutland fisherman, apart from the fact that they are both my countrymen and my fellow beings.

If nevertheless people prefer to maintain that the Jewish race has certain dominating faults—and it is usually the faults the clichémakers stress—other people should be allowed to ask: Why, of all peoples, should the Jews not be allowed to have faults? What justifies the demand that the Jews should be angels?

231

Well, that they have certain faults we do not have, may be the reply. A somewhat hazardous assertion—and like all generalizations dangerous and most frequently unjust. But if we take it for granted that the assertions are correct, would it not be likely then that the faults, which we maintain these people have, have developed by the influence of their surroundings as a result of centuries of exile under the yoke imposed upon them by foreigners, and of expulsions as second-class and less valuable beings into a humiliating and mentally mutilating existence in ghettoes, accompanied by the reduction of their means of subsistence to a few despised jobs? Persecutions, torture, and bloody pogroms, imposed on them by *us*—do let us continue the generalizations—by us the just non-Jews and Christians! Is it not possible that the Jew who wrote as follows is right: *We are a product of the persecutions we have gone through, and not all are lucky enough to be purified through suffering.* Who, then, is to be blamed for the faults of the "Jews," if it is not *we* who have caused them by our persecutions? Generalizations are dangerous and unjust. They can also be unpleasant. We see ourselves with blood on our hands.

If we do not admit our guilt as regards the sufferings inflicted on the Jews, since it is unfair to speak of "us" in general terms, then in return we have to admit that our debt to the Jewish people is far bigger than to any other nation in the world; in reality it can scarcely be measured at all.

The Christian religion in itself is a Jewish movement, emanating from a Jewish Founder, preached by His Jewish pupils. The Holy Scriptures of the Jews form part of the Christian Bible, and a very important one at that. They form part of the spiritual inheritance of every man from his earliest childhood. If a schoolboy is asked which he prefers, the New or the Old Testament, he is very likely to answer that he prefers the Old—with its marvelously vivid and illustrative, pious, moral (and also immoral), exciting, and dramatically moving stories about Abraham, Jacob, Joseph, and David. Israel's prophets, too, give the basis of Jesus' teaching by their preaching of the ethic of monotheism, the unbreakable coherence between religion and morals, God and good.

The Jewish religion has left deep traces in our divine service. The prophets' scriptures and the so-called Songs of David are the basis of much ecclesiastical preaching. The "Aronitic" benediction: *God be with you, God bless you and keep you,* is a dear and indispensable part of Christian divine worship. The Lord's Prayer, Jesus' own prayer, the dearest treasure of the Church and of the individual Christian, is a thoroughly Jewish prayer. There is not a word in it which could not be used by the orthodox Jew. Our very concept of God is in close conformity with that

233

of the Jews, and like it, it has its historical origin in Israel's Jahvism. It is a popular Christian misconception that the Jews are ignorant of the idea of God as the merciful and forgiving Father. Our moral code is conclusively based on that of the Jews, and the Ten Commandments have been the basis of the moral education of Christian children all through the history of the Church. And there is no denying that it is a fact which the Christian Church should always keep in view that Jesus himself was a Jew, deeply rooted in the religion and philosophy of his people. It is exactly as stated by Joseph Klausner, professor in the University of Jerusalem, in his pioneer book *Jesus of Nazareth: There is not one feature in the story of Jesus' life, and not a line in his teaching which is not characterized by prophetical and Pharisaical Semitism.*

It is of very great importance for the fight against anti-Semitism that the Christian peoples realize to what degree our religion comes from the same source as the Jewish, and how identical they are on many important points. For this purpose far greater importance should be attached to the recent study of the history of the so-called Late Judaism.

The widespread delusion that the prevalent Jewish school of thought at the time of Jesus, Pharisaism, constituted a religious decline, a fossilization into a shallow study of scriptures subjected to the letter of the law, has no doubt contributed toward an aggra-

234

vation of the antagonism existing between the two kinds of religion. Judaism as we see it today, is a direct consequence of Pharisaism, and its most essential features are simply identical with it. The pioneer works in this field by Travers Herford, the Englishman, and Foot-Moores, the American, have fully proved that contrary to the current perception Pharisaism marks one of the culminations of the development of religion, and that just around the time when Christianity was founded. Shammai, the orthodox rabbi, Hillel, that deep and gentle spirit, the older contemporaries of Jesus, and Gamaliel, known from the story of the Apostles, for instance (Acts V, 34-39), as the first spokesman of religious tolerance in the New Testament, belong to the great figures of the general history of religion.

Their teachings and activities are a continuation of the preachings of the prophets and are far from opposed to them as some people thought. At the core of Pharisaism is the necessity of holiness: *Ye shall be holy, for I the Lord your God am holy* (Leviticus XIX, 2). It is the demand that religion must be lived, translated, and actualized in everyday life, here and now. Neither faith nor teaching, nor study nor confession will suffice. "What really matters is the life we live, the things we do, every day and every hour." Pharisaism stands for a combination of religion and ethics, probably more consistently carried out than by any other religion. It is the good deed, which is the primary object of all true religion, equally in accordance with the concept of the Pharisees and with that of the prophets. And in the cases where the ritualistic precepts of the Torah, the Pentateuch, the divinely revealed teachings, clash with the demands of the moral code, the former must give way. The idea that "the sabbath was made for man, and not man for the sabbath" (St. Mark II, 27) is expressed in the Talmud, too, as a holy tradition from the great scribes. In one place where manual work is recommended and eulogized it says: *You should rather make the sabbath into a working-day than be a burden to men.*

Jesus lived and died a Jew. His attitude toward the prevalent school of thought, Pharisaism, was not that of a relentless struggle, as many Christians think. He visited the houses of the Pharisees, sat at their tables and had friends among them. The scribe who like Himself placed the double commandment of charity as number one among all the commandments He characterized as not far from the Lord's realm. How can it be explained then that in Matthew, Chapter XXIII, He directs blazing, irreconcilable complaints against the Pharisees? *"Woe unto you, scribes and Pharisees, hypocrites,"* He said, and called them *"ye serpents," "ye generation of vipers," "ye blind guides."* Such language does not agree very well with the words of the Sermon on the Mount that one should love one's enemies, nor with the commandment in Leviticus about loving one's neighbor. If these violent attacks with their tendentious partiality are not a later insertion on the part of the early Christian congregation, determined to damn the Pharisees, they may in all psychological and historical probability be nothing but Jesus' protest against certain abuses and malfeasances within Pharisaism—for that matter the Pharisaical scriptures complain of the same things.

The undisguised discrepancies between Jesus' teachings and those of the Pharisees are well known. However, they may be summarized here: on certain points Jesus breaks with the Law and the traditions of the scribes by His powerful: *But I say unto you!* He did not speak like the scribes who never dared say "I," but like one who possessed authority. In contradistinction to the Pharisees' socially and religiously accentuated Judaism He put forward a demand for the submission of the individual to the commandment of love, often in defiance of all human reasonableness and possibility: You shall love your enemy. You shall not oppose evil. If someone hits you on the right cheek you shall turn the left one. And He addresses the illiterates, the gentle, and the simple, whereas Hillel demands of all believers a certain amount of knowledge of the scripture.

The life of Jesus and His preaching were on Jewish soil exclusively. His disciples shall not go into the way of the Gentiles, but rather to the lost sheep of the house of Israel (Matthew X, 5-6), and therefore He sent away the woman of Canaan because she was

237

a stranger (Matthew XV, 24). As regards many matters of importance He was in conformity with the preachings of the Pharisees. For seventeen years after His death His adherents lived in Jerusalem with His own brother Jacob, and Peter, the apostle, as their leaders. They lived as Jews in accordance with the Law and with only one deviation of importance from the other believers in the temple and the synagogue: they regarded Jesus as the Messiah. It was not until Paul arrived that the differences between Judaism and Christianity led to the breaking off of relations, and a lasting separation and enmity. Through Paul's fight against the Torah, to which he gave the legally misleading name of *nomos,* the Law, Judiasm is provided with the less valuable label of "law-religion," and up to present time this label has been maintained by Christian theology. It is a sad fact that even in the New Testament's love gospel about the Kingdom and peace on earth there is a quantity of material which cannot but cause and keep alive a feeling of dislike for the Jewish people. This holds good, too, of the one-sidedness with which the gospel according to St. John, especially, identifies the opponents of Jesus with the entire Jewish people—a tendentious generalization which can do nothing but spoil the relation between the two religions.

To the Christian it is an almost intolerable thought that in the name of Jesus and under the pleading of His gospel hundreds of thousands of innocent people have been persecuted, tortured, killed, and burned. What Albert Schweitzer has written about the white man's treatment of the Negro in colonial Africa applies to anti-Semitism as well. If the story of the Christian persecution of Jesus' contrymen was collected in one book—as it ought to be, I think—there would be paragraphs we would have to skip for the very simple reason that they would be so terrible that we could not bear to read them. And if a Christian reflected upon the relation between the two kinds of religion it should not be forgotten that a Jew once wrote: *We have poured out ink, but you have shed blood.*

Just as I find that today Judaism is more closely connected with the religion of Jesus than much of the Christianity which adorns itself with His name, I consider it possible that if Jesus were to return to earth today He would feel more at home in many synagogues than in most churches. And if He saw the acts of cruelty which have been committed in His name against His people He would angrily turn His back on the Church. At a big church jubilee a Danish bishop, while he was delivering the festival sermon, asked the question: "I wonder what He, the Man from Nazareth, would say if He entered this church today?" It is a well-advised question indeed. What would *that Jew* say?

All the peoples of Europe and the Western world should constantly and increasingly remind themselves what we owe the Jewish people. Through the civilization to which we belong our innermost thoughts are governed by the Jewish moral code and religion. We are indebted to the spiritual grandees of this despised race in science, art, and poetry: Spinoza, Einstein, Freud, Ehrlich, Bergson, Heine, Mendelssohn, and countless others. Who is capable of measuring what the Old Testament has meant to us, great and small, Christians and non-Christians? In his *Dichtung und Wahrheit* Goethe was pleased to tell again in his own words the legends from the Pentateuch, and in his boyhood he learned Hebrew to be able to speak with the inhabitants of the ghetto in Frankfurt, and to read these beautiful stories in the original language. In a giant work Thomas Mann has recreated the story of Joseph and his brethren. Johannes V. Jensen with tears in his eyes has recalled the Bible history of his childhood, and all through their lives the Danish writers Henrik Pontoppidan and Georg Brandes invigorated their souls by reading the Old Testament.

On Yom Kippur, the Day of Atonement, in October 1943 I went to see David, who that day stayed in his room at the Grabows' house in Buddinge Lane to celebrate the festival as far as possible in conformity with the customs of his fathers. He had invited me to attend the holy service, and I had gladly accepted the invitation. Much work and business made me late. I told David that two small children, whose parents had

240

had to leave them with a family in Copenhagen, were to be taken to Sweden, and I asked him to be ready to leave the country the next day. David had not intended to flee yet, but I shall not forget his delight to get an opportunity to help even while making his own escape. We spent an hour together, and first David finished his devotions. In accordance with the old regulations he wore his prayer shawl, the *tallith,* with the prescribed tassels, the *ziziths,* on the four corners of the shawl.

During the discussion that followed we tried jointly to find an explanation for what was happening in those days, a solution for the eternal problem from the Book of Job: why a God to whom we ascribe omnipotence and love for His creation allows the boundless sufferings which fall on mankind and everything He has created, apparently quite arbitrarily. For David the answer to that question of questions was to be found in the thought of the Lord's almighty power, His sovereign elevation above everything mortal: compare with Him the individual and all human beings are "dust and ashes," His thoughts are as far beyond our apprehension as the sky above the earth. But that is the very reason why we can find consolation in the fact that the last, final explanation of the enigma of life and its sufferings He alone can give, although we do not understand it at present.

In a letter he wrote me a month later in Sweden

David spoke of an event which had impressed him deeply, my wife's imprisonment, and returned to the subject of our discussion:

"Elevated high above all rulers, He exists. He alone rules—He alone controls the stars, the world, the atoms as well as the electrons, everything, He alone. He ignores nothing, He endows every animal, every plant with life and strength, He animates everything and everything is supervised by Him. His noblest gem is the man who stamps His picture with his work. Here human weapons are impotent, sufferings are not sufferings any more, there are no more problems. He alone rules—so magnificently—so magnificently and enchantingly alone. . . . That is the reason why the Book of Job finishes in what we describe as 'an elevated frame of mind,' with an eternity in the middle of life, with an eternal peace and happiness, all amidst the grief and distress of pain."

At the Jewish festival while I sat listening to this boy of twenty it was just as if I could perceive all the depth and tension of the Jewish soul. I had a strange feeling of sanctity and festival in the peaceful room, as if the spirit which had inspired the words of the prophets, penetrated the preaching of Jesus, and been an element of Spinoza's thoughts, was present. Perhaps the parallel with Spinoza was the most striking that day. I do not know if David had read him, but all of a sudden I imagined that through his words I understood the strongly Jewish element of Spinoza's philosophy, the passion of the heart to grasp God through the horror and confusion of life, the *amor intellectualis dei,* which finds the explanation and harmony in an ethical pantheism, the basis of which in Spinoza's soul was the ethical monotheism of the prophets, the belief that there is only one Holy God.

This same feeling of a deep-rooted community in all essentials, in spite of all dogmas and the outer ceremonies of religion, I again experienced a couple of months later when I was the best man for a young Jewish friend I had met at the time of the persecution. His wedding took place in the synagogue in Malmoe. The ceremony itself was inconceivably strange to me, but was penetrated by sentiment and beauty. The local rabbi finished the service by addressing the married couple. The words were verses from the songs of the Old Testament, and he preached about humanity and tolerance, eloquently, fascinatingly, simply and profoundly at the same time, I thought. It was as if Lessing's wise Nathan were interpreting the gospel of humanity in the Jewish synagogue. I could not help saying later on at the reception (which, by the way, was held at a Swedish pastor's) that I should have liked to have heard the same speech by the same rabbi at *my* wedding.

Shortly before my wife and I went home to Denmark after the liberation we had our smallest child

243

christened in the cathedral in Lund. One of the sponsors was a Danish friend of Jewish origin. This was arranged with the explicit consent of the dean, who himself officiated at the baptism.

The sponsors are, according also to the Swedish ritual, strongly advised to see to it that the child is brought up in the Christian faith, if the child's parents should die. If by this is meant the catechism of Luther a difficulty may arise for little Nana's nonbaptized godmother. But the essentials of Christianity can certainly be expressed in many different ways, and not only by the words of the New Testament. I should like my little girl to learn the words by the prophet Micah: *He hath shewed thee, O man, what is good; and what doth the Lord require of thee, but to do justly, and to love mercy, and to walk humbly with thy God.* She must know the Golden Rule. Whether she learns it from the Sermon on the Mount: *Therefore all things whatsoever ye would that men should do to you, do ye even so to them,* or from Rabbi Hillel's negative: *Do not do to others what you do not want them to do to you,* is to me inessential. For both formulas include the words: *Such is the law and the prophets.* The commandment of love in the Old Testament about loving God and one's neighbor is also the great commandment for Christians. I am certain our little girl can make out with those commandments, if she takes pains to learn them, and especially to live up to them.

The Talmud does not really belong in the basic education of a Christian, but it contains a good many sayings which it would be useful and good for a Christian, too, to bear in mind at a sensitive age. *Never forget three things,* says Akabja, the old rabbi, *then you will never become a sinner: Know from whence you come, where you are going, and before whom you shall some day settle your accounts.* Those are words which might be found in the "Universal Religion" which Meir Goldschmidt, the Danish poet, hoped could be created by a unification of liberal Judaism and Christianity without dogmas. But that is probably not too easy for a little girl to understand. Another verse from the Talmud says: *The world rests on three things: Justice, Truth, and Peace.* It sounds very simple, but it will perhaps be even more difficult for her to understand, because she is rarely given a chance of seeing that teaching carried out in life—and the explanation of that kind of dogma will probably be given much more easily by example than by words. If, when Nana grows older, she wants a written "explanation" of this scripture, just as in the proper catechism, I will refer her to the late Swedish chief rabbi, Marcus Ehrenpreis, and I shall finish off by taking the liberty of making his words mine:

Since I heard these words for the first time in my early youth I have passed several examinations, and

245

*not least the compulsory one of life, but I have learned
nothing that was more profound, more true, and more
imperative. I have probably never felt this cry for
justice, truth, and peace so spontaneously as I do today. The world rests on three things: Justice, Truth,
and Peace.*